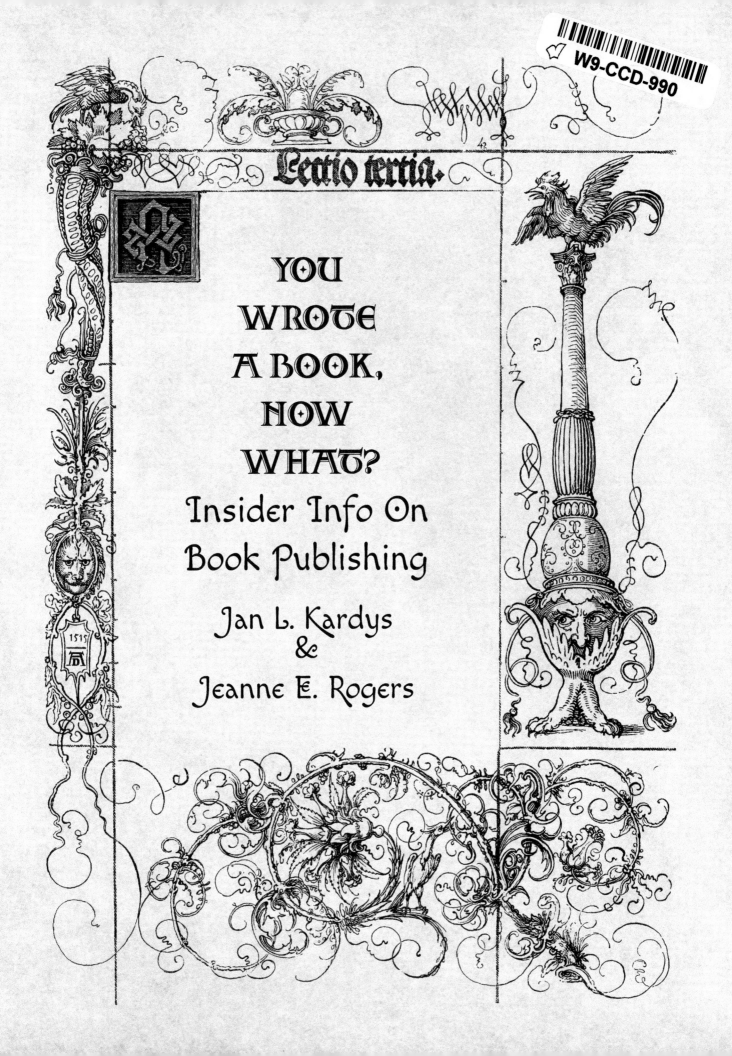

Lectio tertia

YOU WROTE A BOOK, NOW WHAT?

Insider Info On Book Publishing

Jan L. Kardys
&
Jeanne E. Rogers

Book Designed by Annie Sadlon, Abintra Design, Sandy Hook, CT

First Edition – 2014

For permissions or ordering information contact:
Unicorn for Writers LLC, at P.O. Box 176, Redding Ridge, CT 06876.
Email: unicorn4writers@gmail.com.

ISBN:
978-0-9912398-0-1

DEDICATION

This book is lovingly dedicated to our mothers, Dorothea Sweeney Kardys and Helen Gary, two amazing women who will always remain by our sides, in our hearts and in our minds.
They taught us how to love and live well.

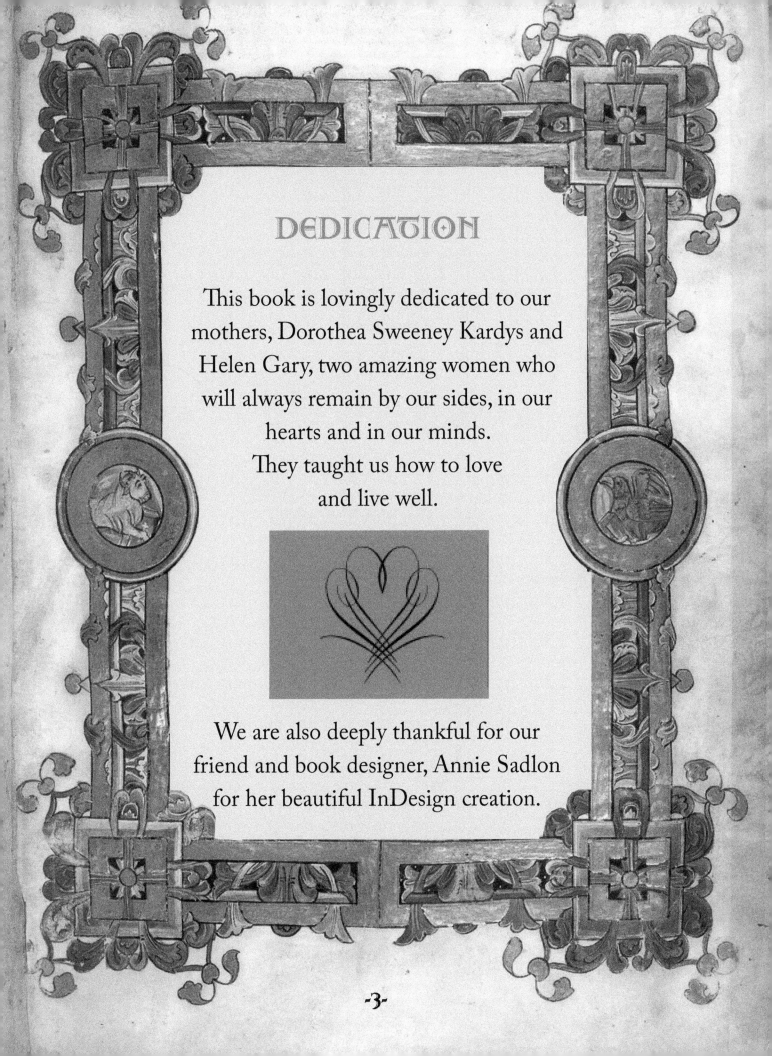

We are also deeply thankful for our friend and book designer, Annie Sadlon for her beautiful InDesign creation.

Authors' Note

You're a writer,
and you've written something
wonderful, but what do you do next?

It's a big question and one that you should
consider carefully. This book was created to provide
writers with the knowledge they need to prepare their
manuscript as well as offer the best assistance in getting
it through or around the gatekeepers of
the publishing world.

You may want to take the route to traditional publishing,
or you may be considering self-publishing. In either case you
will need to understand your options.

You Wrote a Book, Now What? is a practical, and concise
book meant to provide key information and procedures
relative to publishing today.

"The 9 muses are goddesses or spirits
that root from ancient Greek. These goddesses that inspire the creation of literature and arts were considered a pure source of knowledge back in the time. For others they were considered as a 'key to good life', they brought friendship and prosperity as they inspired people to create magnificent things. It was also believed that muses not just inspire the creation of art and literature, but they give hope to people, they help people to behave at their best."
-an excerpt from irema.edublogs.org by irema, January 28, 2010

The 9 Muses are dancing while Apollo is playing the lyre.

Baldasarre Perruzi (1481-1537)

TABLE OF CONTENTS

RESEARCH YOUR COMPETITION

Before you write your book, you should consider one very important question:

"How will my book compete in the market with similar books?"

If you plan on using Literary Agents, Book Editors, or Book Publishers, they will want to know how your book will compete in the marketplace. Bookstores also need this vital information in order to make a key decision as to whether or not they will sell your book. It doesn't matter if you self-publish or sell your book to a traditional book publisher, you need to read, and study the competing books, (what is currently published and in print). In addition, you should know what books are out-of-print. Out-of-print books may be found at libraries or specialty Bookstores. Since a book is a product in the marketplace, you must understand your book's position in the book world. You should prepare a list of at least twenty top competing books that are in print. This information should be formatted as demonstrated below. Prepare a brief description outlining the similarities and differences between your book and others you find in the marketplace.

> Title
> Author
> Publisher
> Copyright date and year of publication
> Price
> ISBN (all versions)
> Number of pages
> Number of illustrations/photographs
> Special features of the book

This task is important because a Literary Agent may request it before or after the Agent reads your query letter or manuscript. Your Literary Agent can use this competition assessment as key information when they approach Book Editors, and Book Publishers.

"Always bear in mind that your own resolution to succeed is more important than any one thing." - Abraham Lincoln

Below are examples for comparison to competing books for *A Thirst for Home*, which is a story about a young girl's transition from the poverty of Ethiopia to life in America. The italicized words indicate the author's thoughts regarding the comparison with the listed books.

Comparison of
A Thirst For Home
by Christine Ieronimo, illustrated by Eric Velasquez, to competing books

Listen To the Wind
Greg Mortenson, Illustrated by Susan L. Roth
Publisher: Penguin Group USA
Pub date: 1/09
ISBN: 978-0-8037305-8-8
Price: $16.99 Hardcover
32 pages, In print
Age range: 5-8, Grades 1-3

This is the adapted children's version of the book *Three Cups of Tea*. It focuses on the lack of schooling and education available in a village in Pakistan.

While my story also touches on lack of education for Ethiopian children, it is not the main focus. It touches on many other issues as well, including unclean water, lack of food, and basic needs. It is Eva's memoir as she recalls what life was like in Ethiopia versus what her life is like now in America.

In The Small, Small Night
Jane Kurtz, Illustrated by Rachel Isadora
Publisher: Greenwillow Books
Pub date: 1/05
ISBN: 978-0-0662381-4-2
Price: $17.99
32 pages, in print
Age range: 4-8, Grades K-5

Abena and her brother have recently been adopted from Africa and find themselves cuddled up together in this strange new bed and tell each other stories so they will not be afraid.

This story takes place over the course of one night as newly adopted siblings tell stories to comfort each other in their new home. There is no discussion about the life they left behind as described in **A Thirst For Home.**

Three Names of Me
Mary Cummings, Illustrated by Lin Wang
Publisher: Albert Whitman & Company
Pub date: 1/06
ISBN: 978-0-8075790-3-9
Price: $27.95
40 pages, in print
Age range: 8-13, Grades 3-8

Ada has three names, one from her birth mother, one from her nanny and one from her adoptive parents. This is a book about self-discovery.

My book has a few similarities to this lovely book. They are both told through the child's voice. They both feel drawn to the country of their birth. They are also similar in the fact that they describe their new adoptive home/family. The major difference is that this story is about a girl adopted from China while my story is a girl adopted from Ethiopia. My story discusses more in depth issues children face that are very unique to Ethiopia. My book also creates more of a dramatic contrast between Ethiopia and America.

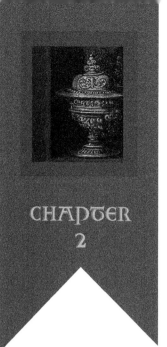

YOUR MANUSCRIPT

Below are recommended suggestions for creating and completing your manuscript for a fiction or nonfiction book. Following these guidelines will help to organize and create a complete and polished manuscript ready for submission to Literary Agents, Book Editors, Book Publishers, Book Printers or a Print-on-Demand Company (POD).

1. Manuscript Creation
2. Manuscript Process
3. Title of Book
4. Manuscript Formatting
5. Manuscript Self-Editing
6. Outline Creation
7. In-Depth Character Analysis
8. Chapter Evaluation
9. One Page Summary
10. Detailed Summary
11. Manuscript Evaluation (Beta Readers)
12. Manuscript Editing (Professional Editors)
13. Manuscript Copyediting & Proofreading
14. Ghostwriters
15. Childrens' Picture Book Setup

1. Manuscript Creation

Use your imagination and dreams to map out the story and structure of your book. Some writers prefer to create a detailed outline that will include the beginning, middle and end. Other writers will simply sit at the computer and begin typing. Explore what works best for you. The major item you need is an idea. However, you also need the passion and writing skills to make that idea come to life on a sheet of paper.

"She had always wanted words, she loved them; grew up on them. Words gave her clarity, brought reason, shape."   -Michael Ondaatje

2. Manuscript Process

There are several software products that writers can use to help them organize and create their manuscript. Two step-by-step story creation software products are Scrivener and StoryWeaver.

3. Book Title

What's in a name, or should we ask, "What's in a title?"
The answer: EVERYTHING!

It is true that your traditional Book Publisher may wish to change your selected title, but you should present your book to Literary Agents and Book Editors with the best title possible. Selecting the perfect title for your book is the first step in marketing your product. Your title sets the tone, and draws the readers into your world, and targets your audience. Finally, your title should entice the reader to want to read your book. Examples of some great titles:

HUNT FOR RED OCTOBER, GONE WITH THE WIND, THE LIGHT AT THE END OF THE UNIVERSE, TO KILL A MOCKINGBIRD, ONE HUNDRED YEARS OF SOLITUDE

4. Manuscript Formatting

HOW TO PREPARE AND PRESENT BOOK MANUSCRIPTS

1.) Print on white 8 1/2 by 11 inch paper.

2.) Double-space your entire manuscript, use black ink and use only one side not both sides (for printing and mailing the complete manuscript).

3.) Type size: 12 pt.

4.) The title of your book, your name and address, email and phone at the top of the first page on the left.

5.) On the right, at the top of the first page, you put the word count and genre.

6.) Title and your author name should be centered on the first page (alone).

7.) Put the book title and your last name on every page of the manuscript to the left, page numbers to the right.

8.) Place your manuscript on a flash drive, computer disk or send via email as requested by your Book Editor or Literary Agent -use the guidelines provided by your Literary Agent.

9.) Each printed manuscript submission should include your manuscript, a cover letter, a self-addressed envelope (SAE), and return postage.

Here is an example of the first page:

The Sword of Demelza/**Rogers**   1.

Jeanne E. Rogers   Approx. 60,000 words
100 Maple Ave.   Middle Grade Fantasy
Anytown, USA 14444
212-333-1111

THE SWORD OF DEMELZA

J.E. Rogers

Here is an example of how following pages should be set up. Your title separated from your last name with a slash, and the page number is part of a header:

Chapter 1

Prologue

The sun was setting over Sunderland and Acadia Abbey. Devon had fallen asleep on the lookout above the manicured grounds. His auburn fur rippled in the summer breeze, and the white star on his forehead gleamed in what remained of the late afternoon sunlight.

He was still young, but he was maturing quickly. Although he was rash at times, he was a strong and clever fox. He loved the monks of the abbey, especially Colum. The old bilby monk had taught him many things about the wild world and soon he would be old enough to leave the abbey and be a part of it. After the tragic death of his mother and father, Colum had taken him in. Devon looked after Colum now that the small mouse-like marsupial was beginning to age. The young fox was dedicated to him and the other monks of the abbey as well. But he often thought of the father and mother he lost. How different life would have been if the tragedy had never happened, if he had never lost them. Still, he was happy here at Acadia. He had all he needed, and life was peaceful. Peaceful, that is, until today.

5. Manuscript Self-Editing

Before you submit your book to anyone, we recommend that you self-edit. Reading your book aloud will reveal issues and errors that you will want to correct for the next version. Deciding how you will self-edit is important. One method is a chapter at a time while you write, and another is completing the entire manuscript and then going back over what you've written. It's a good idea to choose a method and stay with it.

6. Outline Creation

For fiction, the purpose of an outline is to summarize each chapter's plot, setting and character highlights. For nonfiction, an outline will help you organize your subject matter, thoughts and theme.

Some Literary Agents and Book Editors may request chapter-by-chapter outlines for novels, as well as a full synopsis. However, with nonfiction proposals, a chapter-by-chapter outline is essential.

7. In Depth Character Analysis

A good character analysis should describe a character's actions, ethics, motivations, and emotions. It should also describe your major character's behavior and effect on other characters in your story.

An experienced professional Book Editor can help you by creating a concise, thoughtful and useful character analysis for one or more of your characters. In addition, a professional can give you a brief assessment for each character and suggestions for how you can improve them in your book.

8. Chapter Evaluation

We highly recommend that you obtain a review of the first chapter (or several chapters) of your book before you proceed to the next steps. As a writer, you need sound and honest advice about all aspects of these **early chapters** in order to gain insights on how to proceed with your book. You should also reach out to beta readers for their opinions and comments.

9. One Page Summary

A book summary is a comprehensive and concise description of the plot, main points of the book, and major characters. A well-written synopsis succeeds in doing more than just summarizing your book. It attracts and holds the interest of your readers, which includes potential Literary Agents and Book Publishers. The main purpose is to write an enticing summary that will compel the reader to want more.

10. Detailed Summary

A detailed book summary is different from the one page summary in that it is a condensation of the entire story, and is generally composed chapter by chapter. Many Literary Agents require a detailed summary. It is best to be prepared for this possibility in advance.

11. Manuscript Evaluation--(Beta Readers)

You have finally finished your book and you are delighted with the results. You have rewritten it at least a dozen times. The characters are alive in your head, or your nonfiction book conveys the facts just as you hoped, and you long to get published. You feel you are ready to submit your manuscript to a Literary Agent or self-publish. *Is your manuscript ready?* That's the question you keep asking yourself.

Too often writers crash through the gates without really preparing their final manuscript. They assume that a Literary Agent or Book Editor will handle the editing and revisions. This is truly a misconception about book publishing today. Too many times a writer will email submissions and enclosed material, which truly isn't ready for a Literary Agent, and certainly, not for a Book Editor.

To insure that your book is ready for submission to a Literary Agent and/or Publisher, you should obtain honest feedback from other writers, published Authors, Book Consultants and as many beta readers as you can find. Beta readers are not explicitly proofreaders or editors, but can serve in that context. In fiction, elements highlighted by beta readers encompass such things as plot holes, problems with continuity, characterization or believability. In non-fiction, the beta readers might also assist the Author with fact checking, consistency, organization of information, and writing style.

12. Manuscript Editing--(Professional Editors)

After completing your novel or nonfiction book, and after you have obtained feedback from other writers and beta readers, the next step is to find an excellent freelance Book Editor. For fiction, a Book Editor will help you consider the following important factors: characterization (fully developed main and secondary characters), plot structure and sub-plots, climaxes, conflicts, dialogue, point of view, tone, pace, and much more.

For nonfiction book projects a Book Editor will focus on the structure, outline, and direction of your idea and how you should implement it. Also, a Book Editor will carefully study your writing style and give you detailed feedback on how to improve your book.

A Book Editor will carefully and accurately protect the integrity of your book and enhance your final version by offering editorial suggestions and changes. They will help you revise, modify or adapt your manuscript so it is suitable for submission to Literary Agents, Publishers or to prepare it for self-publishing.

13. Manuscript Copyediting & Proofreading (Professional Copyeditors)

Traditionally, a Copyeditor and a Proofreader held separate functions in a Publishing Company. However, a talented Copyeditor will combine these services in order to assist you with your book. The Copyeditor will ensure that the syntax of your writing is smooth, while at the same time he discovers and corrects grammatical errors.

What does a great Copyeditor do for you? A Copyeditor will help you with the following:

Check Grammar	Semantics
Spelling	Fact Checking
Punctuation	Publisher's Style
Jargon	Adding Display Copy
Terminology	Structure

Creativity and critical thinking are involved in copyediting and proofreading your book. You need to get your manuscript into the best condition prior to submission to a Literary Agent, Book Editor, or Book Publisher. If you should decide to self-publish your book, you'll want it to be as close to perfection as humanly possible.

14. Ghostwriters

A Ghostwriter is a professional who writes books, reports, textbooks, or other materials without getting official or legal credit for the work. For some projects a Ghostwriter will completely write the book without any input from the official Author. This work is owned and copyrighted by another person or corporation. An excellent Ghostwriter will spend a great amount of time researching, writing, and editing.

15. Children's Picture Book Setup

If you decide to write a children's picture book, there is formula you must follow. You will have only twenty-four pages in which to tell your story. The image on the following page will show you exactly how a children's picture book should be set up.

SELF-ENDED PICTURE
BOOK LAYOUT

I

COVER

YOU HAVE TWENTY-
FOUR PAGES TO TELL
YOUR STORY

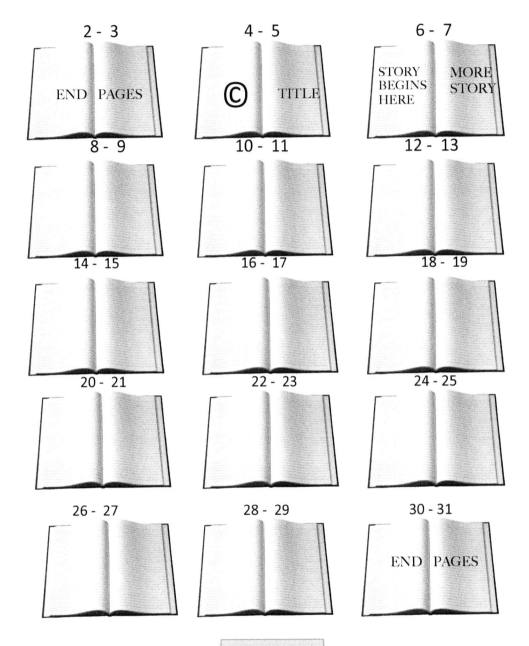

2 - 3

END PAGES

4 - 5

© TITLE

6 - 7

STORY
BEGINS
HERE

MORE
STORY

8 - 9

10 - 11

12 - 13

14 - 15

16 - 17

18 - 19

20 - 21

22 - 23

24 - 25

26 - 27

28 - 29

30 - 31

END PAGES

In a 32 page picture book, you don't actually have 32 pages for your story. You only have 24 pages since 8 are used for the bookends, copyright and title.

32
BACK
COVER

And 24 pages translate to 12 spreads (an illustration can span two pages or there can be an illustration on each page.)

TRADITIONAL VS. SELF-PUBLISHING

As you dream of publishing a book, please keep the following things in mind:

1.) You'll need to research your **competition.**

2.) You'll need to insure that your manuscript is in perfect condition for submission to Literary Agents or Book Publishers.

3.) You'll need to find the right Literary Agent. You can do this by creating a winning **query letter** about your book and an excellent **summary** of the book.

4.) You'll need to learn how to approach, submit, and develop your **"pitch"** to a Literary Agent, Book Publisher, and your targeted book buyer.

5.) You may need to write and submit a **marketing plan** for your book.

6.) To improve your odds of becoming published, you'll have to learn to analyze the editorial interests of Book Publishers by studying their online catalogues.

7.) It is vital today to understand the publishing business and contractual considerations with all the different self-publishing companies and traditional Book Publishers before you sell, market, and promote your book to the public.

Publishing Consultants

Whether you are a new writer or a seasoned published Author, there are numerous questions and issues you will need to address before becoming a part of today's changing publishing arena. It may be wise to consult with Publishing Professionals/Publishing Consultants before you approach a Literary Agent, Book Editor or Book Publisher.

Book Printers

Finding the right printer is important if you self-publish. Many new writers will not do the research necessary in order to find the appropriate printer for their book. Research includes the printer's work history, background, printing submission guidelines, bindings, paper samples, and the printer's minimum print runs. For example, if you use the wrong printer the binding might be weak and will not hold the book pages together properly.

"Nothing stinks like a pile of unpublished writing."   - Sylvia Plath

Understanding the complex print world is challenging and can be costly if an inappropriate printer is used for your book.

Today, you can use a traditional book printer such as **R.R. Donnelly,Bookmasters, Courier, McNaughton Gunn, Inc., Worzalla,** and **Webcrafters,** or a print-on-demand house such as **Lulu, Vervante, Blurb, Lightning Source, Smashwords,** or **CreateSpace.** There are many different options. You must carefully investigate the costs, printing quality of the materials used, and the financial structure for any printing company you decide to use for your book. In all cases, your book must be available for sale on **Amazon** and **Barnes & Noble** sites.

Book Distributors

Book Distribution is the method of getting your books from the printer to the reader. The key to your success as a published Author is finding the right Book Distributor for your book. A traditional Book Publisher will not allow you to sell your book in a book-store without using their sales force, and they have Book Distributors that they have worked with for years. However, if you self-publish you have many options: personal website, Amazon (an on-line Book Distributor), Baker & Taylor, Ingram, Content Group, Perseus Books Group, and many other major and small Book Distributors.

A great Book Distributor may be expensive, but they can reach many sales channels, i.e., online retailers, bookstores, libraries, academic institutions and other outlets. Book Distributors handle all the hassles of credit card transactions and order fulfillment.

Self-Publishing Checklist

1. Research the Competition.

2. Edit your Manuscript and Copyedit the Final Version.

3. Copyright your book with the US Copyright Office.

4. Start collecting quotes from published authors.

5. Create your Publishing Company (LLC) or publish under your name.

6. Obtain an ISBN, Barcode Number (www.myidentifiers.com
R.R. Bowker).

7. Obtain a Tax Permit Number for your Publishing Company/Federal ID Number.

8. Proofread your book one last time for errors and read one last time before you print.

9. Find a Printer via Literary Marketplace, Volume Two or online.

10. Prepare your Cover and interior design. You will want to seek out a book designer. (You need a Work-for-Hire Agreement for cover art or interior book design. See Chapter 15 on Resources for an example agreement).

11. Negotiate an agreement with the printer for costs, due dates for books, type of paper, binding, trim size, hardcover or paperback, following their specific guidelines.

12. Consider cross marketing web links on your Website or Blog. You can do this by sharing other Author's links on your site, and having your link placed on their site.

13. Create email lists of potential book buyers, and send out an email to them.

14. Google Book Search is an excellent tool for promoting your book. You can scan in the entire book, or a few chapters and make it a part of Google Book Search.

15. Send your book for reviews. ***Publisher's Weekly, Kirkus, Library Journal, Amazon*** reviews, related magazines (ask a librarian for lists of magazines that will review). Create an Ad Campaign, and Press Release for your book. Contact local radio stations, Internet shows, and TV shows to highlight your book. Create specialty items such as postcards, bookmarks, and other print material to advertise your book.

16. Marketing on the Web is a must and can be accomplished through a myriad of social media venues such as: Facebook, LinkedIn, Goodreads, Google+, ads in magazines, genre contacts (for example romance book - associations/organizations - advertising, contact romance authors via blogs or websites).

17. Be prepared to hold special events in libraries, schools, colleges, book stores, companies and organizations. Consider your audience and then prepare a presentation to focus on the most important aspects of your book.

18. Consider attending Book Expo and Writers Conferences. You will learn a great deal as you network with other Authors and speakers.

19. Talk to people in a bookstore about your book, and try to line-up an in-store signing.

Below is a table, which highlights some of the main differences between self-publishing and traditional publishing:

	SELF-PUBLISHING	TRADITIONAL BOOK PUBLISHER
MANUSCRIPT TO EDIT	Writer must self edit or obtain outside editor for final & complete manuscript	Recommend that you edit your book carefully before submitting to an agent however, editor in a publishing house is responsible for editing your final manuscript
QUERY LETTER TO AGENT	NO need to send out	YES
SUBMISSION GUIDELINES AGENTS	NO need to follow	YES
SIGN ON WITH A LITERARY AGENT	Agent not needed	YES
COPYEDITED MANUSCRIPT	YES, you must have your manuscript copyedited and proofread before you publish	Your Book Publisher will handle
OBTAIN ISBN and BARCODE	YES, you must obtain an ISBN & barcode/Bowker	Your Book Publisher will handle
COPYRIGHT FORM	YES, you can obtain a form via the US Copyright Office	Your Book Publisher will handle
INTERIOR ART	YES, you must find an artist	Your Book Publisher will handle
COVER ART	YES, you must find an artist and book designer to assist you	Your Book Publisher will handle
FREELANCE AGREEMENTS	YES, work-for-hire agreements with editor, copy editor, artist, and book designer for interior of book	Your Book Publisher will handle

	SELF-PUBLISHING	TRADITIONAL BOOK PUBLISHER
PRINTER	You must find a printer and negotiate a good print deal	Your Book Publisher will handle with their printers
WAREHOUSE BOOK DISTRIBUTOR	You may want to consider a Book Distributor, you must store books	Your Book Publisher has book distributors and warehouses
SALES FORCE	You must handle your own sales	Your Book Publisher will handle
PROMOTION	Your job	Some Book Publishers will support their authors and actively promote their books
ADVERTISE	Your job	You will appear online and in the print catalog of your Book Publisher
MARKET	Your job	Publisher should make recommendations
WEBSITE	You are responsible for having a website	Your Book Publisher will not write or program your site
BLOG	You are responsible for having a blog	Your Book Publisher will not create or write your blog

	SELF-PUBLISHING	TRADITIONAL BOOK PUBLISHER
SPECIAL SALES	Your job to sell in these markets. Without contacts, it is difficult	Your Book Publisher will attempt to sell special sales, and premium rights
SUBSIDIARY RIGHTS	Your job to sell in these markets. Without contacts, it is difficult	Your Book Publisher will make good efforts to sell/ license these rights
EVENTS	Your job to obtain events to help sell your book	Your Book Publisher can make some great suggestions for you

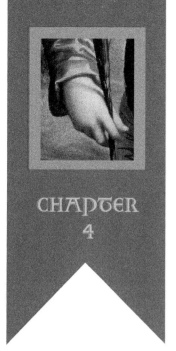

CHAPTER 4

NONFICTION BOOK PROPOSAL

Book Proposal Review

For writers of nonfiction, the book proposal is the key to publication. In many cases, the book proposal is written before the book itself, and will determine whether or not the Author is contracted with a Book Publisher or Literary Agent. You might wish to use a Publishing Consultant to evaluate and critique your book proposal. The consultant will review your written material and proposal. Is your idea solid? Is your formatting attractive and effective? Is your argument clear? Is your proposal an accurate reflection of your work?

How To Write a Book Proposal - Submission Guidelines

Cover Letter -Must include return address. Should not be longer than one page. Briefly explain why you are writing to the agent or editor in question--for instance, does he or she work with authors whose writing resembles yours? Be sure to offer a one to two sentence description of your book. For example: "My novel is the Latina ***Coldest Winter Ever.***"

Overview -In two or three paragraphs, describe your book's content and purpose. What gap does it fill in the market, if any? For nonfiction, what need does it fulfill, or what problem does it solve? Include supporting statistics, if relevant. For instance: "The fastest growing sector in the U.S. for small businesses is not only women, but Latinas."

Author Biography -Focus on relevant information regarding your education, credentials, experience, awards, and achievements. If you write fiction, have your poems or short stories appeared in journals or won awards? Do you have an M.F.A., and if so, which program did you attend? Do you know well-established writers who would give your manuscript a glowing pre-pub quote? Have you published any other books? If so, provide name of publisher, publication date, and--most importantly--sales for each previously published book, including those that were self-published. Did your past books garner positive reviews? Were book club and foreign language rights sold? Did your past books win awards, or appear on bestseller lists? If your work has only been published outside of the U.S., indicate the country, or countries, in which it has been published. Are you an acknowledged expert on the topic on which you book is written?

"Sweet words are like honey, a little may refresh, but too much gluts the stomach."
- Anne Bradstreet

Does your writing regularly appear in magazines, newspapers, or online? Do you have a syndicated column? A radio or television show? Are you the creator of a popular website, and if so how many hits on average does it receive?

How You Will Help Sell Your Book - Selling your book is not just your publisher's job--it's also yours. Do you regularly hold seminars, workshops or lectures at which the book could be sold? If you do, approximately how many speaking events do you present a year, and approximately how many people attend each event? What kind of organizations do you speak for (i.e. Fortune 500 companies, universities, non-profits, etc.) Do you have any contacts with the media--television, radio, newspaper, magazine, Internet --that would be helpful in promoting the book? Are you willing to hire a publicist at your own expense to complement the publicity efforts of your publisher? Have you ever founded or are associated with a relevant organization? Do you have a database of clients/members/fans to whom the book could be sold? Do you plan on buying a large quantity of books at a discount to resell? If you have a web site, will you promote your book on it? If not, will you create a website to help promote your book?

Competition - List the books in print that most resemble your book, preferably those that have sold well. Describe how your book differs from each, and how that difference will help make your book sell as well, if not better. For example, if you've written a low-fat Mexican cookbook, every other low-fat Mexican cookbook in print is competition. If there aren't any direct competitors, list the books in the same category that come closest; in this case, regular Mexican cookbooks. Note: There is no such thing as a book with no competition. Every book published on the same subject and located on the same shelf as your book in a store is, technically speaking, competition.

Specifications - Approximately how long is the final manuscript in terms of word count? For novels, do not submit a proposal until the manuscript is complete. For nonfiction, if the manuscript is incomplete, how much time do you need to finish it? Have you already shown it to other editors and/or agents If so, what was the outcome? Indicate whether the book will include any special features, such as illustrations (color or b&w, photos or line art), tables, sidebars, excerpted or reprinted material, etc. Note: Authors are usually responsible for supplying art as well as obtaining and paying for permission to use art and/or reprinted material.

Synopsis/Table of Contents - For fiction, include a short (no more than three pages) synopsis. For nonfiction, include a complete table of contents with a brief paragraph describing each chapter. Indicate if there will be a resources section, appendix, bibliography, etc.

Sample Chapter - For both fiction and nonfiction, provide only one sample chapter, preferably one that best represents not only your writing ability, but also the book's basic premise. If you wrote your manuscript in Spanish, have at least a chapter of your work translated into English by a translator you trust. Do not send an entire manuscript unless the editor or agent has specifically requested that you do so.

SASE - Always include a self-addressed stamped envelope (SASE) large enough to contain all the material you wish returned to you. It is not appropriate to enclose cash or checks to cover postage. Though rare, submissions are occasionally misplaced, so do not include original art or anything of value that cannot be replaced.

Clippings - Include copies (not originals) of recent clippings about you and your work. For instance, if you were quoted in an article by a local paper, include a copy of the article. If you've ever appeared on television, network or cable, include a video. Include clippings and/or videos even if they are in Spanish.

Presentation - Don't use fancy binders, covers, plastic comb binding, etc. When editors/agents get excited about a proposal, they need to Xerox it and share it with colleagues as quickly as possible, and fancy binding gets in the way. Save your money and use rubber bands, paper clips and/or binder clips instead.

Used by permission of Marcela Landres. Contact: **http://www.marcelalandres.com/**

Please note that the above submission instructions are general and not specific. If you are planning to submit to a particular Literary Agent, Book Editor or Book Publisher, you should obtain their specific submission guidelines and follow them to the letter.

QUERY LETTERS, SUBMISSION GUIDELINES, AND HUNT FOR A LITERARY AGENT

CHAPTER 5

How to Write a Query Letter

Purpose: Your Sales Pitch to Hook a Literary Agent

A concise and well-crafted query letter describes your book in the most succinct and intriguing way possible. You may query several Literary Agents simultaneously but make sure you email one agent at a time. If there's interest in your book, the Literary Agent will request additional information, such as your book proposal, sample pages, and/or the complete manuscript.

A professional, 1 to 1½-page query letter sent via mail or e-mail is your first written contact with a Literary Agent. If sending by mail, a self-addressed, stamped envelope (SASE) for return of materials is required including sufficient postage for return of your printed manuscript. Your query letter should contain:

- A compelling sentence that pitches your book
- Fiction/Nonfiction
    - a) Fiction: Genre, main characters, setting and plot should be mentioned in the letter
    - b) Nonfiction: Genre, description and proposed number of illustrations/photos
- Brief bio for both fiction and nonfiction, and for nonfiction a brief explanation why you are qualified to write the book
- Concise information about the competition and market for this book
- Description of your previously published articles and books, if applicable
- Enclosures: Published articles, table of contents, bio credentials - which help the sale of your book
- Contact Information: Your name, e-mail, fax, phone numbers and address

You must avoid arrogance, spelling, punctuation and grammatical mistakes in your query letter. Carefully proofread your letter before you email it to a Literary Agent.

Always follow the agency's submission guidelines before sending a Literary Agent a query letter. Do not send the same query letter to several Literary Agents in the same Literary Agency. If you are submitting your manuscript to a Book Publisher who is accepting unsolicited manuscripts, be sure to follow their guidelines, as well. Unsolicited means that you can send your manuscript without having a Literary Agent.

"The very existence of libraries affords the best evidence that we may yet have hope for the future of man." - T. S. Eliot

Sample Query Letter

Dear Agent,

Nestled in the rolling hills of Sunderland, Acadia Abbey is home to the bilby monks, mouse-like marsupials who built the abbey. When his parents are killed, Devon, a young red fox, is adopted by Colum and raised at the abbey. One day, Flitch, a vicious thylacine, attacks the abbey with a group of dragon lizards. Colum is killed and Devon leaves the abbey with a single minded purpose; revenge. Meanwhile, in the small hamlet of Digby, a poisonous brown snake attacks a family of marsupials. Edlyn Grassley is bitten as her twins, Erik and Emma, look on in horror. With instructions they receive from Aldon, a powerful sorcerer and Guardian of the Forest, Erik and Emma, embark on a quest to collect ingredients for a potion that will save their mother's life.

A chance encounter brings Devon, Erik and Emma together. Although they are natural enemies, they forge an unlikely friendship after learning that an evil king, named Cynric has gained control of a powerful sword. With this sword, he is setting the countryside ablaze, and killing defenseless forest creatures. The friends decide to set aside their personal goals and join a rebel army dedicated to ending his reign.

In a fierce final battle beneath the towers of Fortress Demelza, Devon and Cynric come face to face with their past. Locked in mortal combat, Cynric recognizes his son who he believed was dead. As Cynric dies, Devon takes possession of the sword, and peace is restored to Sunderland.

At 62,000 words, The Sword of Demelza is a fast paced middle grade adventure that can be compared to Brian Jacques' Redwall series, or Warrior Cat series, but additionally educates as it entertains. The book contains moral lessons about courage, family loyalty and tolerance of others. It also introduces young readers to the unusual flora and fauna found only in Australia. A glossary at the end of the book, and a link to a website showing pictures of the actual animals enhance the educational goal of the book. It is fun for young readers and an educational tool for teachers.

I am a member of the Connecticut Authors & Publishers Association, the New England Society of Children's Book Writers and Illustrators, and the Society of Environmental Journalists.

Thank you for your time and consideration. I look forward to speaking with you, and would be happy to send the completed manuscript at your request.

Sincerely,

Jeanne Rogers

Sample Query Letter

Dear Agent,

Mere moments after Bella the Snowflake tumbled from a polar-bear-shaped cloud, she turned into a world-class diva. She just 'knew" she was the most beautiful snowflake in the sky and nobody, not even that bi-polar bear cloud, was going to tell her otherwise. Bella soon learns that she is one of billions of other ordinary snowflakes. She couldn't tell where she ended and they began!

The Most Beautiful Snowflake is an enchanting story set in a winter wonderland populated by sparkling characters. It is a funny, entertaining, simple story with a not-so-simple message. Like Bella, even though we are individuals, we are also part of the whole of humanity. Bella comes to realize and finds joy in recognizing that she is a very important part of an exquisite snow cover upon the countryside.

Children who hear the story are captivated and fall in love with Bella. The story stands the test of telling time and again.

I am the author of Rap-Notes: Shakespeare's Greatest Hits, Vol 1, the Fringe NYC Festival musical play, The Seed of Abraham, a dozen one-act plays, and more than a hundred radio and TV commercials. I also wrote, directed and edited the American Film Festival award-winning documentary, Nadine Valenti, Portrait of a Painter.

At your request, I will send the manuscript of my 700-word book picture book, *The Most Beautiful Snowflake.* I think you'll see why it would be so appealing for children, ages 5 to 7, as well as their parents. I hope to hear from you soon.

Sincerely,

Bob Zaslow

Here is a list of some traditional and untraditional ways of finding a Literary Agent.

- *Publisher's Weekly* - weekly magazine and Literary Agents' big deals are in the magazine
- *Literary Marketplace* - listing of Literary Agents
- Writers Conferences - *Shaw's Guide to Writers Conferences* http://writing.shawguides.com
- Recommendations from published Authors - meet at book signings
- Acknowledgment pages in books mentioning Literary Agents' names
- Find similar books in the bookstore or library and check to see if the book is in print. Call the Contracts Department or Permissions Department of the Book Publisher, and ask who the Literary Agent is for the book (select Authors in the same genre as your book)
- Recommendations from list of Literary Agents at *Unicorn Writers' Conference*
- *Publishers Marketplace* - Internet website currently $25 per month
- *2014 Guide To Literary Agents* by Chuck Sambuchino
- Jeff Herman's *Guide to Book Publishers, Editors, and Literary Agents*
- *Writer's Digest Magazine* - writes often about Literary Agents
- QueryTracker.net and AgentQuery.com– Internet search tool for Literary Agents

Literary Agents

If you want to publish your book through traditional channels, it will be necessary to find the right Literary Agent. Many new writers will not do the research necessary in order to find the right Literary Agent for their book. Research includes: the Literary Agent's background, submission guidelines, and area of interests. The number one reason the aspiring writer gets rejected is because the writer has approached an Agent who is inappropriate for his/her book. Understanding the complex publishing world is challenging. Even if you do find the perfect match, you need to know *who, when and how* to approach each Agent.

Publishing Executives or experienced Publishing Consultants have the contacts and the knowledge to provide you with a detailed list of Literary Agents that are appropriate for your book. In addition, the Publishing Consultant should document the reasons for selecting each Literary Agent. Generally, you only need Literary Agents who have experience selling books to Book Publishers who will publish books similar to your book's genre/subject matter. There are always exceptions to the rule.

Submission Guidelines

Below are examples of the submission guidelines for Curtis Brown and Black Hawk Literary Agency. Every agent's requirements are different. Before you send a query letter, be sure to follow the guidelines of that particular agent.

Curtis Brown

Curtis Brown represents adult and children's authors of all genres, including illustrators. If you would like to submit a manuscript or proposal, please send us a query letter, a synopsis of the work, a sample chapter and a brief resume. Illustrators should send 1-2 samples of published work, along with 6-8 color copies (no original art).

Please enclose a stamped, self-addressed envelope for our response and return postage if you wish to have your materials returned to you. We typically respond to queries within 6 to 8 weeks.

Please send all book queries to:
Curtis Brown, Ltd.

Attn: Query Department

Ten Astor Place
New York, NY 10003

• We do not charge reading fees.

• We do not handle stage plays or musicals.

• We are not accepting screenplay submissions at this time.

• We regret that we cannot guarantee the return of submissions sent without a self-addressed, stamped envelope.
Copyright © 2008 - 2012 by Curtis Brown, Ltd.

Black Hawk Literary Agency

Query letters may be sent via email to: SubmissionsJanKardys@gmail.com
Please send a query letter of no more than three pages, which includes your credentials or biography and a detailed explanation of what makes your book unique. Please explain why there is a market for your book.

Manuscripts Mailed: Kindly include a self-addressed stamped envelope for our reply, which generally takes six to eight weeks. Email submissions are required and only on special written request will printed manuscripts be accepted.

Guidelines for fiction: 1. Plot synopsis. 2. Previous publishing history (if any). 3. Paragraph about yourself (bio).4. Contact information: name, address, phone, fax, and email address.

Guidelines for nonfiction: 1. Synopsis, along with relevant history of the subject or your expertise in that subject area. 2. Previous publishing history (if any). 3. Paragraph about yourself (bio). 4. Contact information: name, address, phone, fax, and email address.

To expedite my comments: If you audiotape the first six chapters and send it to us on a disc, we may be able to respond within three weeks. If your material interests us, we will request the entire printed manuscript. Printed manuscripts take longer to review.

EBOOK PUBLISHING

An **electronic book** (variously: **e-book, eBook, e-Book, ebook, digital book,** or even an **e-edition**) is a book-length publication in digital form, consisting of text, images, or both, readable on computers or other electronic devices. Although sometimes defined as "an electronic version of a printed book," many eBooks exist without any printed equivalent. Commercially produced and sold eBooks are usually intended to be read on dedicated eBook readers, however, almost any sophisticated electronic device that features a controllable viewing screen, including computers, mobile phones, and nearly all smartphones, can also be used to read eBooks. There are various devices for reading an eBook - Amazon's Kindle, Barnes & Noble's Nook, Sony Reader, Kobo, Apple's iPad, iPhone and iPod, and others.

Changes-Impact on Publishing Today-Future

The eBook has made a surprising impact on the publishing world. It's not enough to have a book in print. It is now important to have your book available in eBook format as well. In fact, the experts predict that eventually, there will be more eBook editions sold than print editions.

Author - Publishing Agreements Electronic Rights

Depending on the Book Publisher or company handling an Author's electronic rights, it is important to understand what an Author is granting to the Book Publisher concerning electronic rights before the Author signs an initial book publishing agreement.

Electronic Display - Electronic Multimedia

Generally, electronic rights will include electronic display rights as well as multimedia rights. For example, an enhanced electronic version could be interactive and embedded with audio, video, animation, sound effects, and other enhancements.

Example of a Publishing Agreement's eBook Editions Clause

"If published as an electronic text (eBook) or electronic audio (e-audio) edition, 25% of the net amount actually received from such sales. However, should marketplace

"It is with words as with sunbeams, the more they are condensed, the deeper they burn." - Robert Southey

conditions change such that said royalty rate is below prevailing market rates, Publisher agrees to renegotiate the royalty rate at Author's request at any time following three years after first publication of the eBook edition. On Publisher's exercise of electronic adaptation rights granted herein the royalty rate shall be the prevailing rate paid for similar uses. The parties shall negotiate in good faith to establish such rate.

However, if an Electronic edition is not sold by the Book Publisher, the Publisher may license rights (as a Subsidiary Rights) to another party or e-publisher and the split is 50% to book publisher and 50% to the Author. In addition, a Publisher may license electronic excerpts of the book to another party or publisher."

The above is the eBook and audio clause in a major New York City Publisher's agreement.

Formatting to eBook

Formatting a manuscript in preparation for an eBook requires extensive work. Companies like **CreateSpace** or **Lightning Source** have the capacity to do so. There is a cost associated with this process.

COPYRIGHTS, PERMISSIONS, RELEASES, WORK-FOR-HIRE

CHAPTER 7

1. Copyrights

"Copyright" is the legal protection of a creative work. Using a work without permission that is under copyright is against the law. Creative works are protected for 95 years (if published before 1978), or the life of the creator of the work, plus 70 years, if published after January 1, 1978. Remember, the work is the property of the person who created it. To use it without permission is stealing.

You need to complete the copyright certificate for your self-published or unpublished book with the US Copyright Office. The website is: **www.copyright.gov**.

Authors, Book Editors, and Book Publishers understand the need for a thorough review of a manuscript in order to prevent legal controversy, libel, and copyright infringement.

The copyright page is where an Author will note where portions of the book have been previously published, permissions to publish extensive excerpts, quotations from copyrighted works, and photo credits.

The copyright notice consists of three parts: the symbol ©, the year the book is published, and the name of the copyright owner. It is a practice of many Book Publishers to use both the word "Copyright" and the symbol ©, but either is acceptable.

Example: Copyright © 2015 Deborah Sweeney
All rights reserved. Published 2015.
Printed in the United States of America

2. Permissions

If you plan on using material in your book that comes from another book, magazine, newspaper, website, lyrics, or any other source material, you must obtain written permission from the copyright owner to use that material. The only exceptions are *fair use* and *public domain* material.   See **http://www.copyright.gov/fls/fl102.html** for explanation of fair use. See **http://www.copyright.gov/pr/pdomain.html** for an explanation of public domain.

"A well-composed book is a magic carpet on which we are wafted to a world that we cannot enter in any other way."   - Caroline Gordon

If you wish to you use an excerpt from a published novel, you will have to look at that book's copyright page. On that page you will find the publisher, title, Author's name, and copyright notice. This will give you the source to contact in order to obtain permission to use that excerpt.

Here is a checklist for obtaining permissions. This information is needed by the copyright holder before they grant you permission to use their material.

• Title of the book and Author's name
• Exact excerpts, chapters, page numbers, paragraphs, specific lines, number of words
• Copyright page from publisher's books or material
• Title of your book and Co-Authors
• Your Book Publisher's name
• Title of your publication
• Circle those that apply:

Mass Market	Newspaper
Textbook	Electronic book
Magazine	Website
Newsletter	Other

• Your book's publication date
• Cover price
• Number of pages
• Territory; world in all languages, world in English, or United States, Canada and its territories (USCP)
• Changes, adaptations, and condensations must be approved by publisher and Author
• No additions or added or substituted artwork without publisher's consent
• Use for subsequent editions
• Use in a book club will require an additional fee
• Excerpts used are not assignable or transferable
• Publisher's credit notice will be printed in your book

You should look at Chapter 15, "Resources," for a Sample Permissions License.

3. Releases

If you take a photo of people in a group (private citizens who are attending a public event), you will need to obtain a signed release form before you use the photo for publication in your book. If you take a photo of someone under eighteen, you will need a signed release from that person's parent. At times you may not have to pay a fee to include these photos in your book.

You should look at Chapter 15, "Resources," for a Sample Photo Release License.

4. Work-for-Hire

A Work-for-Hire Agreement is an agreement in which services with another person are provided for an Author or Artist. All rights remain with the Author or Artist. A Work-for-Hire Agreement contains all the details, terms and conditions necessary to protect you, the Author, with another party, such as, a freelance Book Editor, Copy-editor, Proofreader, Typist, Book Designer, Artist, Book Indexer, Book Printer, and Book Designer. Under a Work-for-Hire Agreement, you the Author, do not give any rights and/or copyrights to the freelancer or other party.

You should look at Chapter 15, 'Resources,' for a Sample Work-for-Hire Agreement, which you can alter for any of the above services.

AUDIO

CHAPTER 8

Audio Recordings

According to the Audio Publishers Association, the total number of audio books published in the last three years has doubled. This is an additional source of income for self-published and traditionally published Authors.

Many major Book Publishers wish to obtain audio rights in order to license them to an Audio Publisher. The split is generally 50% to the Book Publisher and 50% to the Author, and there are some special exceptions in the splits. The percentage allocated for the Author will be paid to the Author or Authors' Literary Agent only after the advance paid for the book has earned out, and at times, an Author might never see any income from this sale (in the case where the advance is unearned). See Advance & Royalties in Chapter 15 for more information.

If a Literary Agent retains these rights on behalf of the Author (the Agent's client), the Literary Agent should attempt to sell these rights to an Audio Publisher. However, there are only a few Literary Agencies that have one or more persons devoted to exclusively handling the licensing of audio book rights for all their Authors at that agency.

An experienced publishing expert will focus on these important rights, and either request a reversion of rights for unlicensed rights from a Book Publisher, check on the status of your existing audio licenses, review your audio rights royalty statements, contact your Literary Agent to get the ball moving on licensing these rights, and/or focus on selling these audio rights for you.

As an Author (unpublished or published), you can excerpt up to 15% of your book and use it on your blog and/or website to help promote your book. However, if you are a self-published Author, you do not have any restrictions on the amount of material you excerpt from your book in audio form for use in promoting your book.

"I try to create sympathy for my characters, then turn the monsters loose."
- Stephen King

Audacity® is free, open source, cross-platform software for recording and editing sounds.

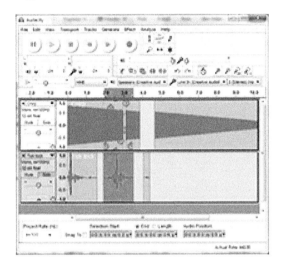

Audacity is available for Windows®, Mac®, GNU/Linux® and other operating systems.

Create an Audio Book

You may want to consider having your book made into an audio book at ACX. At ACX.com you can hire a professional to read your book. There are a number of options and costs associated with creating an audio version. Check out the details on ACX.com.

An Amazon Platform

About ACX   How it Works   Promote Yourself   Need Help?

About ACX

You're Empowered
A Marketplace For You
Earn Money With Audiobooks
How You Benefit
Know Your Rights
Who We Are
What's The Deal?

How It Works

Authors
Authors As Narrators
Narrators
Print Publishers
Audiobook Publishers
Agents
Studio Professionals
Video Lessons & Resources

How It Works

Calling all authors, narrators, agents, publishers and studio pros: ACX needs you!

Are you ready to revolutionize the audiobook creation process? Here are step-by-step instructions of how ACX works for you.

Authors

Get your title up and out there:

○ Confirm your rights

○ Create your title profile

○ Find a Producer

○ Make a deal to get your audiobook produced!

CHAPTER 9

SALES, SPECIAL SALES, SUBSIDIARY RIGHTS SALES

Sales

A Traditional Book Publisher will have a sales department and sales representatives sell your book to bookstores, libraries and other traditional book markets.

Traditional sales channels consist of the following:

Bookstore national chains	Library wholesalers
Bookstore regional chains	Internet retailers
National wholesalers	Independent bookstores

Special Sales

A **special sale** is selling a book outside the traditional trade book marketplace.

Special Sales are made up of the following channels of distribution: Specialty Retail, Mail Order (Direct Response), Specialty Wholesale, Educational Wholesale, Display Marketers, Premium & Corporate Sales, and Custom Publishing/Proprietary.

A **premium** is a book or audio that is used for promotional purposes. Premiums are often sold to corporations who are looking to add value to a product or to bring product awareness to consumers. Premiums are used as corporate gifts, promotional giveaways, gift-with-purchases, or as a purchase-with-purchase.

Many major Book Publishers have a Special Sales Department for their frontlist* and backlist* titles. Self-published authors do not have the experience necessary in order to sell their books in these markets. In the event you have been published by a Traditional Book Publisher and can obtain a reversion of special sales and/or premium rights, these rights and books can be promoted and sold in these non-traditional marketplaces. An experienced Special Sales consultant may license or sell your books in these markets.

*Frontlist: The new titles in the marketplace, just published and less than one year old.
*Backlist: The titles that have been in print for a while.

"I read so I can live more than one life in more than one place."
- Anne Tyler

Subsidiary Rights

Subsidiary Rights are ancillary rights that are granted by an Author to a traditional Book Publisher who will license various rights to another party or Book Publisher (for example, first serial rights, second serial rights, book club rights, reprint rights, large print rights, audio rights, electronic display rights, electronic multimedia rights, paperback rights, foreign rights, British rights, and other subsidiary rights). Generally, a major publisher has a Subsidiary Rights Department, which controls and licenses these rights for the Book Publisher on behalf of the Author. There are various income splits between the Author and Book Publisher once the book advance has earned out, and at the next royalty period the Author receives their allocated share of the subsidiary rights income. For example, the split for second serial rights are 50% to the Author and 50% to the Book Publisher. If the serial rights sale to a magazine is $1,000 (after the book advance has earned out), the Author will receive $500 and the Book Publisher will receive $500. However, 15% of the Author's share will be allocated to the Author's Literary Agent.

In many large Publishing houses, the Subsidiary Rights Department may review a manuscript before an offer is made to the Author's (or Artist's) Literary Agent in order to determine the potential subsidiary rights income. This helps the Editor or Book Publisher estimate the advance and the number of copies they anticipate they will sell in the market. A complete flow through clause of subsidiary rights income means that the Author will receive the Author's share of the subsidiary rights income regardless of whether or not the advance has earned out.

An experienced Publishing Consultant has the experience and knowledge to license these rights for self-published Authors, and/or to advise traditionally published Authors on subsidiary rights in their publishing agreements before the contract is signed with the original Book Publisher. If the original book publishing contract has been fully executed, this consultant can advise placement of these rights and possible amendments to reacquire any rights not exercised.

Below is a list of terms relating to Subsidiary Rights:

First Serial — Excerpts of the book before publication (major Literary Agents generally retain these rights to sell for their Authors) to magazines and newspapers (some major publishers with strong connections to leading magazines will negotiate to retain these rights).

Second Serial — Excerpts of the book after publication to magazines and newspapers. Note: The Author's share of first serial or second serial rights is accounted against the advance, and once the advance has earned out, earnings start to flow to Author's Agent. Agent will receive the check from the Publisher and take out the Agent's commission, generally 15%.

Syndication — Syndication to New York Times Syndicate, LA Times Syndicate

Anthology — Selections or the entire book in an anthology or commercial or academic version

Large Print — The entire book is sold to a Large Print Publisher

Library Edition — Sold in the library marketplace

Deluxe Edition — A more expensive edition of the book, leather bound, for instance

Selection — Excerpts of the book

Abridgment — Either the entire book or excerpts of it

Condensation — Publisher licenses the right to sell a condensed version of the book, for example, to Reader's Digest

Digest — For example, Reader's Digest

Adaptation — Adapting the book and licensing to another party or Publisher

Graphic Format — Graphic excerpts or edition to a magazine or Publisher

Educational Media — Educational media edition to another Publisher or for in-house use

Educational Edition — A derivative work, for example, to another Publisher or for in-house use

Microfilm

Microfiche

Electronic — (Electronic display, electronic multimedia, eBook) Agent may split these rights and offer only the Publisher electronic display without changes in the text of the book. Publishers will want a limit on the numbers of words released in order to promote the book electronically, and be concerned about first serial rights to an online magazine.

Audio — Audio edition of the book to another audio Publisher or for in-house production

TV and Motion Picture — Generally retained by the Author's Agent to license

Merchandising — Mugs, calendars, t-shirts, etc., generally retained by the Author's Agent to license

PUBLISHING AGREEMENTS & BOOK PUBLISHERS

Finding the right Book Publisher is one of your main objectives. You can use a Literary Agent to sell your book to a traditional Book Publisher, and negotiate a book deal with that Book Publisher, or you can submit your manuscript to Book Publishers who will consider your book without being represented by a Literary Agent.

Many new writers will not do the research necessary in order to find the right Book Publisher for their book. Research includes the Book Publisher's list of titles (front and backlist), submission guidelines, and area of interests. The number one reason the aspiring writer gets rejected is because the writer has approached a Publisher who is inappropriate for his/her book. Understanding the complex publishing world is challenging, and requires time consuming research and consideration. Even if you do find the perfect match, you need to know who, when and how to approach each Book Publisher and the right Book Editor at each Book Publisher and each Publishing house. Generally, your Literary Agent will find the right match. The alternative would be finding a Book Publisher who will accept an unsolicited manuscript.

A seasoned Publishing Consultant has the contacts, and the experience to provide you with a detailed list of Book Publishers that are appropriate for your book. In addition, they should document the reasons why they selected these Book Publishers. You need recommendations from those Book Publishers that are a match to your book's genre/subject matter.

Book Publishers

Who are the major Book Publishers?
- Penguin Random House
- Simon & Schuster
- HarperCollins Publishers
- Macmillian U.S.
- Hachette Book Group
- Harlequin
- Kensington
- John Wiley & Sons, Inc.
- W. W. Norton & Company
- The Perseus Books Group

"The past is always tense, the future perfect."
- Zadie Smith

All of the above have many divisions and imprints, generally organized by category and genre of the books that they publish, distribute, and market. In addition, several of these New York Major Book Publishers are under the control of a massive, parent-media conglomerate. For example, publicly traded News Corporation Limited owns HarperCollins and CBS Media owns Simon & Schuster.

Publishing Agreements

As a published or self-published Author you will need to either prepare or review various agreements related to your book. Please take publishing contracts seriously and read the fine print. Such contracts might include, publishing agreements, or work for hire agreements with freelance editors, copyeditors, web designers, programmers, artists, and other parties. If you are published you may need a reversion of rights letter (or a partial reversion of rights agreement). You may need to request a cancellation and return of advance documents. You may be considering a subsidiary rights agreement with a foreign publisher, or special sales agreements.

A skilled Contracts Director/Publishing Consultant will have a wealth of experience drafting, negotiating, and revising a comprehensive range of contracts for wide variety of publishing rights. These rights could involve U.S., U.K., and other jurisdictions. They may include adults' and children's book agreements, contributor agreements (for illustrators, photographers, translators, and designers), co-edition agreements with museums and galleries, co-publishing arrangements, reprint and other subsidiary rights, electronic and audio agreements. This could be a very difficult area to navigate without assistance and the appropriate protection.

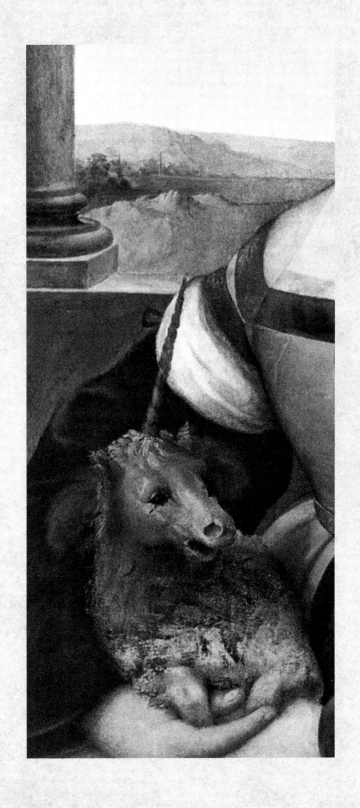

MARKETING & PROMOTION

What Does Marketing & Promotion Mean To You?
It Means You Must...

Capture your target readers with massive exposure

Create excitement about your book before it is published

Customize your marketing plan for your book

Today, many Book Publishers expect a Literary Agent to include an Author's marketing platform along with the book proposal or manuscript. Why the change in the book industry? For one, the book market is saturated with self-published Authors who have been forced to learn how to market and sell their own books.

Learning from the success of these self-published Authors, major Book Publishers now believe that their Authors should take on this responsibility. This is an unspoken reality. Your Book Publisher will include your book in their printed and online catalog, their sales force will attempt to sell your book, and the Publicity Department will send your book out for magazine and newspaper reviews. Creative marketing with innovative ideas and marketing strategies for your book will depend upon the few people assigned in the Marketing and Publicity Departments in various publishing houses, unless you:

> Can do **bookstore, organization** and **library events**, read portions of your book, and provide a service to the community in a book-signing event.

> Can organize with other published authors and share the expenses for a **special book event** tied with some entertainment in your town.

> Do **online marketing** through social networking sites.

> Maximize free advertising from other readers and published authors by word of mouth.

"Happiness is an accident of nature, a beautiful and flawless aberration."
- Pat Conroy

Obtain **Amazon's recommendations** and great book reviews from the public. ("People who bought this book also bought...")

Author Quotes

It's wonderful to include blurbs, endorsements, or quotes from Published Authors with your submission to Book Publishers. If you can't get a famous Published Author to provide a quote on your book, try to find someone who is an authority in your subject area. These quotes are generally printed on the back cover or inside jacket of the book. If you prepare a press kit for your book (at your own expense, if your Book Publisher doesn't plan on spending the money), include these endorsements in your kit.

Social Media

The Internet has changed the way people communicate. It has also changed the way people market themselves and their businesses. Selling your book is a business and knowing how to use the Internet to your advantage is absolutely necessary if you are to promote yourself and your book successfully.

Your first task is to gain credibility and influence, become known, and create a platform on which to build your business and later, create ancillary products.

As Facebook, Twitter, Pinterest, Goodreads, YouTube, LinkedIn, and other social media sites expand with new users daily, more Published Authors are turning to these sites to create electronic chatter prior to a book's release. This is how a self-published Author will attract a loyal audience and increase sales. Social media lets you connect to your target audience in a way that is quick, easy and often free.

You need to develop a strategic plan customized for your book using top social media sites and marketing concepts with instructions to expedite your plan. Cross-marketing and detailed marketing plans will assist you in maximizing media coverage.

Media Training

Readers want to personally know Authors. In order to market your book properly, you will need to be able to speak about it and yourself. If you get nervous and fumble when speaking in front of people a media trainer can help. If you don't know how to handle a radio or TV interview a media trainer will show you how.

A Media Trainer will give you valuable insight on how to pitch your book and how to engage and hold the interest of your audience. A Media Trainer will teach you how to effectively introduce yourself, and how to pitch your book in two magical sentences. However, you should also learn how to train yourself to speak clearly and with confidence, flair, focus, and poise.

Book Publishers today demand that a prospective Author possess strong presentation skills, and you must become proficient in the art of the broadcast interview as well as a variety of public speaking venues.

Marketing Platform

In general, major Book Publishers do not have time to market and promote your book. However, your book will appear in their online or print catalog, and on the Book Publisher's website. A Book Publisher's sales force will attempt to sell your book to various bookstores and chains, but there are many limitations on what each major Book Publisher can do for your book. Unless you are a best selling Author, a major Book Publisher will not assist you in marketing your book. Please look in the Resources section at the back of this book. You will find the Authors have included their own marketing plan, which includes a checklist to help you develop your own.

Essentially, your marketing platform or plan should cover these categories:

1. Print
2. Internet (website/blog, podcasts, YouTube)
3. Special Appearances and Special Events
4. Radio
5. TV
6. Social Media

Book Trailers

A book trailer is an exciting way to advertise your book. A good book trailer will engage and entice your potential readers. In other words, book trailers, or book videos are a great way to promote you and bring attention to your books. It's an easy and inexpensive way to reach your target audience.

You will be able to use a book trailer to generate book sales through video-sharing sites (YouTube), websites, social-networking sites, blogs, and any book related sites on the Internet.

You should work closely with an experienced and talented expert who will produce an affordable book trailer for you.

PowerPoint Design

A wonderful way to capture your audience is with a PowerPoint presentation for use at a library event, or during your promotional tour for your book. Simply take your laptop and projector on the road and connect with your potential book buyers. Open the show with a stunning presentation, which organizes your message, excerpts your book, and delights your attendees.

Tag Line

A tag line is a short, simple and tight slogan for your book. Your tag line is important to your brand, genre, and provides essential information about your book, and it is imperative that you develop a good tag line.

Jacket Flap Copy

Your jacket flap copy gives potential readers an exciting, brief summary of your story. Its purpose is to hook the reader, and entice them to purchase your book. Flap copy is an important selling tool, and it should be concise, well written and intriguing. If you are considering self-publishing your book as a soft copy only, you will need flap copy for the back of your book.

Book Reviews

An excellent review of your book can generate excitement. It can also create more fans, and book sales. There are many different ways to obtain reviews. Consider looking for reviewers on Facebook, LinkedIn or Goodreads.

Catalogue Copy

In traditional publishing Catalogue Copy appears in the on-line and print versions of Book Publishers' lists of books. It is key information for bookstores, libraries, and on-line companies such as Amazon and Barnes and Noble. The Catalogue Copy should include the following items:

Cover of the book	Marketing Plan
The title	Publicity
Sub-title, if any	List the number of illustrations -
Author's name	black and white and color
Key Selling Points	10- and 13- ISBN numbers
Summary of the book	Price and the format
Very brief author bio	(hard cover, paperback, audio, eBook, etc.)
Author's residence	Publication month

If you are self-publishing, all of this information can be used to help you create your own 'sell sheet,' which you can hand out to bookstores and libraries.

Creating Your Brand

This is the home page for Unicorn for Writers, the authors' website.
(http://unicornforwriters.com)

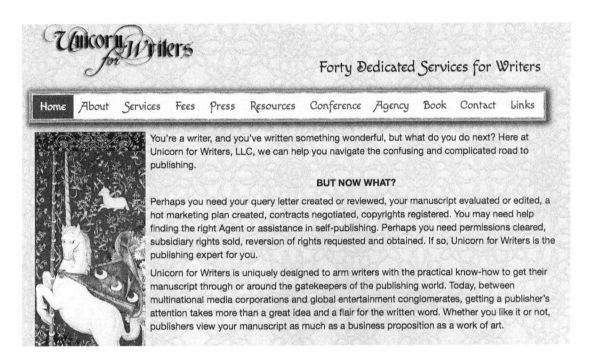

You can see the establishment of our brand, which includes the scripted letters 'Unicorn for Writers' along with the image of the unicorn from the Portiere Licorne tapestry. You should make every effort to establish your brand for yourself and your books.

Unicorn for Writers LLC
unicornforwriters.com

ART

Whether you are a self-published Author seeking interior or cover art, or a published Author who wishes to enhance your website with illustrations, selecting the appropriate artist is key for your success.

Book Cover Design

You can judge a book by its cover, and most readers do.

"The cover of a book is akin to the door of a home; if it is welcoming, and interesting, it makes the visit all the more pleasurable and desirable."
J. E. Rogers, Author

The book jacket and cover of your book is your reader's first impression. It is an important image that should impress your public. You want your readers to be drawn to your book, and it's your book cover that will help achieve this goal. ***You want your book cover to stand out, display your professionalism, convey the message of the story, and clearly express the genre, and age group you want to reach.*** Your cover must captivate and charm your potential audience.

Many Authors focus on their manuscript, but forget about having a cover that complements and effectively shares the value of its content. Knowing your intended audience, and what will appeal to them, will guide your decisions for a successful cover design and text.

Illustrations

Some of the most important books in the world are also stunningly beautiful. They have become iconic masterpieces in their own right. The outer and inner make up the whole.

Some books, due to their subject matter, require illustrations. Other books are simply enhanced by them. Illustrations help readers associate words with objects, and clarify the author's message by bringing that message to life, with a drawing. You should consider whether or not your book would be improved by including illustrations.

Picture Book Art Review

You've written a picture book and illustrated it.

"Prose is architecture, not interior decoration."
- Ernest Hemingway

The rules for creating a picture book are very specific, and you will need to learn the format for a thirty-two page children's book, as well as what you can expect relative to submitting a picture book with art to potential Book Publishers and/or Literary Agents. See Chapter Two for the thirty-two-page picture book set-up.

INTERNET

Website, Blogs, Podcasts, Internet Radio, YouTube, Cross Marketing

CHAPTER 13

Website Layout & Design

A website is an important component of your Author platform. You should be planning a website well in advance of publishing your manuscript.

So, what should you be considering? Who is your audience? What information, and what message should your website contain? When creating a website, you need to think about the information you want to convey to your potential readers. Should you use images, an author picture, bio information, contact information and/or event pages? How many pages should you have on your site and should you add audio and media?

The layout of a web page is usually what people think of when they begin to create web design. If the layout is poorly planned, doesn't work well, or doesn't convey the right message to your readers, then your readers won't stay on your site. You need to know what web design works; what keeps readers interested and intrigued enough to stay, and return.

Authors need some key headers for their website and blog in order to attract readers. You need a publishing consultant and a programmer with experience in website design and layout. This is your logical first step before the website is programmed using a template, free website service, or a professional software package.

Here are a few examples of Author websites. Note all the common tabs:

> **http://jodyhedlund.com/books/preachers-bride/**
> **http://www.karenrobards.com**
> **http://www.tchevalier.com/index.php/books**
> **http://nicholassparks.com**
> **http://www.jamespatterson.com**
> **http://annerice.com**
> **http://sandrabrown.net**
> **http://www.celestinevision.com**
> **http://www.elizabethgilbert.com**

"The secret of getting things done is to act."
- Dante Alighieri

Podcasts

A podcast is a type of digital media consisting of an episodic series of audio, video, PDF, or ePub files subscribed to an downloaded through web syndication or streamed online to a computer or mobile device. The word is a neologism derived from 'broadcast' and 'pod' from the success of the iPod, as audio podcasts are often listened to on portable media players.

Internet Radio

Internet radio involves streaming media. This media presents listeners with a continuous stream of audio that cannot be paused or replayed. In this respect, it is distinct from on-demand file serving. Internet radio is also distinct from podcasting, which involves downloading rather than streaming. Many Internet radio services are associated with a corresponding traditional radio station or network. Internet-only radio stations are independent of such associations.

Blogs

The word 'blog' is a contraction of the word weblog. Blog sites are information sites published on the worldwide web, which contain posts of interest to the blogger and hopefully to the blogger's readers. For example, there are many blog sites whose subject matter focuses on writing and grammar. Author blogs have developed in recent years and help individual Authors highlight their passions and writing ability. On these blogs, readers can communicate with the individual Authors by leaving messages or reacting to the posts published by the Author.

CHAPTER 14

Business Cards, Postcards, Bookmarks, Printed Excerpts

One of your first tasks as a writer is to learn how to effectively market your creation. A large part of that marketing task is networking with potential book buyers in order to successfully sell your book. Your key to making a first and lasting impression must be a strong one. This first impression will become your brand, and it must reflect you and your book. Business cards, postcards, printed excerpts (first 25 pages), and bookmarks can become your initial calling cards. Make sure that they are well thought out and designed.

A publishing expert will help you to creatively design, according to your written specifications, your special brand.

Stickers, Banners, Brochures, & Promotional Materials

Creative and fresh ideas are essential and one way to approach this is to consider your book as a product. Consider having some stickers created for your book cover. If you have been honored with an award you can apply that seal to your cover. If you have a children's book, you could create stickers of some of your characters for a coloring book or sheet.

Many nonfiction books or even novels could benefit from printed opening pages or excerpts, which could be placed in a brochure or booklet. These could be given out gratis to potential book buyers. In addition, some books will be ideal for ads placed in the appropriate subject related magazine online or in print. For example, if you write a book about animals, you may want to consider an ad in an animal related magazine.

You can also create lens cloths, tablecloths, mugs, shirts, calendars, mouse pads, notebooks, bookmarks, etc. Or you can license merchandising/commercial rights for your book.

"If you can tell stories, create characters, devise incidents, and have sincerity and passion, it doesn't matter a damn how you write." - Somerset Maugham

Below is a list of just some of the many promotional materials available:

Postcards	Car Magnets	Flyers
Bookmarks	Rack Cards	Calendars
Business Cards	Labels	Booklets
Printed Excerpts	T-Shirts	Tablecloths
Stickers	Mugs	CD/DVD Package
Banners	Posters	Table Tent
Brochures	Letterhead	Tent Cards
Magnets	Notepads	Window Decals

CHAPTER 15

RESOURCES

Important Resources:

Books in Print	Shaw's Guide
Library of Congress	Amazon.com
US Copyright Office	Authors Guild
Google Book Search	Publisher's Weekly
Beyond the Book	Barnes & Noble
Copyright Clearance Center	Book Expo
Literary Marketplace	Google Products
Writer's Digest	Facebook
Publishers Marketplace	YouTube

Publishing Terms:

AA - Author's Alternatives -Changes made by an Author after type has been set and a charge is made to the Author's account or paid directly to publisher by Author

AAP - Association of American Publishers

ABA - American Booksellers Association

ABI - Advanced Book Information - R.R. Bowker collects information from Book Publishers for inclusion in their books Forthcoming Books and Books in Print.

Advance - A sum paid to the Author on signing of the publishing agreement with the Author. An advance is generally applied against (deducted from) royalties or other sums due the Book Publisher. Agents take out their commission from the advance and all royalties earned.

Association of American Publishers - The trade association of the largest book publishers in the United States.

Auction - The sale that gives several Book Publishers the opportunity to bid on the rights to publish an Author's book and held by a Literary Agent. The book goes to the highest bidder.

Backlist - Previously published books that are in print. Front list books are recently published books.

Bar Code - Identification and price marking in bar format on books, generally placed on the back of the book. The bar code for books is called Bookland EAN.

Bio - This is the background information about the Author, work, and other experience that helps promote the book.

Book Club Rights - Rights to sell a book through a book club.

Book Packager - Packagers create the book for Book Publisher, from manuscript to finished book, or a combination in between.

"To produce a mighty book, you must choose a mighty theme."

- Herman Melville

Buzz - The word-of-mouth excitement created in the publishing industry before a book is released.

CIP - Cataloging in Publication data - Bibliographic information supplied by the Library of Congress that is printed on the copyright page. The CIP data aids libraries to index the book

Deal Memo - A short letter of agreement (one page) between the Book Publisher and Author's agent that precedes the Author agreement but contains advance, royalty rates, subsidiary rights, territory, and option clauses.

eBook - A book that is not available in printed form, only in electronic form.

Editorial Board - A group of people who collectively make the decision to buy and publish a book. Also, called Pub Board. Editors present book proposals or manuscripts to the editorial board for its approval.

Electronic Editing – Online editing is an editing process for a manuscript, including copyediting, re-writes, proofreading, and indexing, on a computer instead of paper.

Electronic Rights - Subsidiary rights dealing with electronic, multimedia formats (i.e, the Internet, CD-ROMS, electronic magazines).

Fair Use - The allowable and legal use of a limited amount of copyrighted material without getting permission.

Flap Copy - Text inside covers of the book.

Floor Bid – Book Publisher offers to enter a floor bid when the book goes to auction (to other competing publishers). The Book Publisher sits through the auction but agrees to take the book by topping the highest bid, by an agreed upon percentage- (usually 1%).

Foreign Rights - Translation rights and rights sold abroad (French language rights, British edition, etc.).

Hook - Aspect of the work that sets it apart from other books.

ISBN - International Standard Book Number - The ISBN identifies the book.

Net Receipts - A type of royalty payment based on the amount of money a Book Publisher receives on the sale of the book after the book seller's discounts, special sales discounts, and returned copies.

Option Clause - This clause gives the Book Publisher the right to publish the author's next book in which the Author briefly outlines the book.

Public Domain - Creative works that are no longer protected by copyright law and may be used by anyone without permission or further payment.

Remainders - Leftover copies of an out-of-print book purchased at a reduced rate.

Slush Pile - A stack of unsolicited submissions in the editorial office of a Book Publishing company that wasn't represented by a literary agent.

Subsidiary Rights - Rights included in a book contract. Some are always granted for the publisher to handle, including second serial rights, book club, paperback rights, permissions, electronic display, large print. The Literary Agent negotiates the remaining subsidiary rights and either sells them for the Author or allows the Book Publisher to handle them.

Synopsis - A ten to fifteen page summary of a novel, written in third-person, present tense. It explains the plot of the novel in an effective, analytical, and concise way.

Work-for-Hire - An arrangement in which the Author is paid on time for work, and the Author does not own the copyright to the work.

Here are some issues and considerations you should think about and discuss with your Literary Agent before the book deal is offered:

Working Checklist

Author/Publishing Contract
Author: _____
Title: _____
FIRST FORMAT: HC( )PB( )Other( )
ISBN HC: _____
ISBN PB:_____
ISBN BIG BOOK: _____
ISBN Paper on Board: _____
AUDIO ISBN: _____
Other ISBN: _____
eBook ISBN:_____
Advance: $ Payout: _____

Joint Accounting (standard) ( ), or Separate Accounting ( )

Bonuses: $
Specify: New York Times ( ), Newbery Award or Honor ( ),
Printz Award or Honor ( ), National Book Award or Honor ( )

Permission Grant to Author**: $ (**Publisher to pay the Author to offset the costs of obtaining permissions, provide payout of money and timing of such payout.)

Series Language Required In Contract:

Is the book part of a new series or existing series? _____
Did the series originate with Publisher or with Author? _____
Territory: WORLD: in all languages WORLD: in English
US, Canada, Phil & non-exclusive Open Market excluding B.C.
US, Phil, & Open Market (no Canada) excluding B.C.
US, Canada, Phil only (no Open Market)
US & Canada only (no Open Market)
US, Canada, Phil & non-exclusive Open Market excluding British Commonwealth
  & Europe/Union (approval of Publisher required & not recommended)_____
MS Due Date*: Word Length:
(*Multiple deliverable – specify please)

Description of Work:_____
Option (EXPLAIN): Yes No detailed proposal detailed proposal and sample chapters.

If the Work is derived from TV, Movie or Trademarked property, does Publisher have right to use title, logo, trademarks, special photos from? Yes No
_____

Photographs: Yes No Paid by Author/Artist? Explain: _____
_____

Illustrations: Yes No Paid by Author/Artist?
Explain: _____
Charts/Diagrams: Yes No Paid by Author/Artist?
Explain: _____
Permissions/Releases: Yes No Paid by Author/Artist?
Explain: _____
Copyright in the name of the Author? Yes No
Competitive Works/any concerns: Yes No
Will Author or Author's affiliated company commit to buy stock of book as part of deal? Yes No
Will Author revise the Work for next edition (no additional advance)? Yes No
Special Provisions

Advance and Royalties

A Book Publisher pays an advance when signing a publishing agreement with an Author (or artist) for the rights to publish your book.

An advance is a sum of money (usually half is given when you sign a contract, and half is given when you submit the manuscript), and it is generally applied against (deducted from) royalties, subsidiary rights income, and other sums due the Book Publisher. Think of an advance as cash given to you before your book starts making money. Until your advance has earned out, you won't receive royalties from your book sales.

Carefully check every royalty statement that comes in before you call the Royalty Department and complain about missing money. Ask your Literary Agent if he or she has reviewed it as well. If you obtain copies of all of your subsidiary rights contracts (not your permission licenses) and the appropriate subsidiary rights royalty statements, you will be able to figure out income from subsidiary rights if your Book Publisher bundles all the sub-rights money on a statement.

You should have the right to audit your Book Publisher at least once a year with a CPA. In general, it is traditional that your Literary Agent handles any problems with incorrect money owed (overpayments or underpayments) on the statements.

EXAMPLE OF ADVANCE AND ROYALTIES

Advance: $20,000
Price of book: $20
Royalty rate on hardcover book: 10% of retail list price
Author earns $2 per book sold through normal retail channels. To earn out the $20,000 advance, the publisher will have to sell 10,000 copies of the book.

The payment of the advance is generally half on signing of the publishing agreement between the Publisher and Author, and half on acceptance of a complete and satisfactory manuscript. However, there can be variations of the payout of the advance: one third on signing, one third on acceptance of the manuscript, and one third on first hardcover publication.

A contract for multiple books will have a different payout. An Author should not have to pay back an unearned advance. A clause stating this should be added to your publishing agreement.

Since book stores can return books they purchased and get their money back, in most cases, a Book Publisher will hold a reserve for returns from an Author's first royalty statement. Every Publisher's reserve for return policy varies: one might hold back 30% on the first three accounting periods, whereas another might hold reserves on all statements.

Royalties and Royalty Statements:

Standard book royalties:
Hardcover: 10% to 5,000 copies, 12.5% to 10,000, 15% thereafter
Trade paperback: 7.5% for all copies sold
Mass-market paperback: 8% to 150,000 copies, 10% thereafter

SUBSIDIARY RIGHTS:
(consult or approval with Author on any subrights)

SUBRIGHTS	AUTHOR'S SHARE	PUBLISHER'S SHARE	CONSULT	APPROVAL
First Serial	90%	10%		
Permissions & Reprint	50%	50%		
Electronic Display	50%	50%		
Electronic Multimedia	50%	50%		
Commercial	50%	50%	Should be Retained by Author	
Foreign	75%	25%		
Translation	75%	25%		
Dramatic	75%	25%	Should be Retained by Author	

SOFTCOVER ROYALTIES:

SOFTCOVER	AUTHOR	
Standard: 8%		
Book clubs: 6%		
Book fairs: 6%		
Dividends: 3%		
Mail Order: 5% Amount received		
High Discount: 5% Amount received		
Overstock: 10% Amount received		
Export: ½ applicable Royalty HC/PB		

HARDCOVER ROYALTIES:

HARDCOVER	AUTHOR	

10% on 1st 5000 sold

12 1/2% on next 5000 sold

15% thereafter

Sample Permission License (From A Publisher)

Name
Address
City, State, zip code
Re: ___by ____
Title_____ Author_____

Dear _____

Thank you for your permission request dated _ for the above- mentioned title for use in your print publication____. Permission is hereby granted in the English language throughout the United States and Canada only for your excerpts from our book for the sum of $___ which is due within 45 days of signature of this permission license. This permission is limited to the text of the book and exclude any other material (il-lustrations, photographs).

You agreed that you will credit the Publisher in the following manner:
"Reprinted by permission of___from____(title)
By __(Author) Copyright © 20_ by AUTHOR. ALL rights reserved."

It is understood and agreed that the rights granted are not assignable or transferable and apply only for the specific material and for your publication. In the event this excerpt is used in an electronic edition you will reapply for permission.

This permission license will terminate if any terms of license are violated. In addition, the license shall terminate if the above fee has been paid within 45 days of the date this license.

Please sign all copies of this license and return one copy with your payment. Also, send two copies of your work to the attention of ___upon publication. Thank you.

Sincerely,

Permissions Department

Releases

If you take a photo of people in a group (private citizens who are attending a public event), you will need to obtain a signed release form before you offer the photo for publication in your book. If you take a photo of someone under eighteen, you will need a signed release from that person's parent. Often you don't have to pay a fee for including these photos in your book.

Photo Release Request Form

I am writing a book to be published by _____, tentatively entitled_____. I am writing to request permission to include the above-mentioned photographs in my book. Enclosed is a copy of the photograph(s) I want to use. Will you kindly grant permission for the use of such photograph(s) in any and all editions and versions of my book and any derivations thereof throughout the world? We will include the appropriate copyright acknowledgement or credit line. Would you kindly sign below to indicate your acceptance and return this letter to me? Thank you.

Sincerely,

Your name here...

I hereby grant you the permission requested above. I warrant and represent that I am the owner of the rights granted herein and that the material does not infringe upon copyright or any other rights to another person, party, and/or rights holder.

Copyright Acknowledgement/ Credit line:

_____

Photographer Printed Name

_____

Accepted and Agreed to by Rights Holder/ Photographer's Signature:

_____

Work-for-Hire

Agreement made this   day of   2014, between

("Editor"), whose address is   and

whose address is

(the "Author"), regarding services of Editor with respect to:

(1-   "the "Work").

This Work-Made-For-Hire Agreement is hereby commissioned by the Author with the Editor for ordered work and services in accordance with the Author's specifications defined as follows:

To give Author a detailed list of changes of least 25 pages of suggested changes on each page, and to edit the entire manuscript.
Payment is 1/3 on signing, 1/3 on delivery of 75 pages and 1/3 on delivery of final changes.

(the "Book").

Editor undertakes to perform such commission on behalf of Author and to deliver the Book in form and content satisfactory to Author no later than   2014, time being of the essence.

The parties agree that the Book prepared under this Agreement shall be Work-Made-For-Hire. To the extend that said Book may not qualify as a work-made-for-hire under U.S. copyright law, it is nonetheless agreed that the Editor hereby transfers and irrevocably assigns all right, title and interest in and to any material by Editor hereunder to Author, including but not limited to all copyright rights of every kind, nature and description, including world-wide copyright and renewal rights, derivative works, in all languages, and the right to register the copyright to the Book in the name of Author or Author's successors, designees, licensees and transferees. All right, title and interest to any material prepared hereunder by Editor in connection with the Book shall, at all times, and regardless of the state of completion, by owned by Author. Nothing contained in this Agreement shall be construed to obligate Author to make any use of the Book whatsoever or to prohibit Author from making any changes or alterations to the Book as Author, in its sole discretion, may elect. In the event the Author elects not to publish or use the Book, such Book shall be owned and remain the property of the Author.

Author shall have the right to use any such material prepared by Editor hereunder in the Work, in any future editions of the Work, and in any other publications, works, or programs in all forms and media without any further payment to Editor unless otherwise specified in this Agreement.

As full consideration for all of Editor's services and for the exclusive right of Author, its assignees and licensees to use the Book in the Work and in any other publications or works, in all forms and media, Author shall pay to Editor the total sum amount of: _____

Editor is entering into this Agreement as an independent contractor and shall not be considered as Author's employee, agent or co-venture, and is not entitled to participate in any benefit plans for Author's regular employees. It is understood that Editor will have no right or authority to make any commitments on Author's behalf.

Editor represents and warrants that the Book will be Editor's original work for Author's use, and that its preparation and publication will not violate any copyright or any personal or proprietary right. Editor agrees that said Book and the obligated defined herein will not be in conflict with other publishing commitments, or prevent the use of the Work and other services. Author shall be solely responsible for obtaining any permission required for the Book and shall deliver such permissions, in writing, upon delivery of the Book. The use thereof will not be libelous or infringe or violate any right of copyright, privacy, or any other right of any person or entity.

Neither this Agreement nor any rights under this Agreement may be assigned, licensed, sub-licensed or otherwise transferred by Editor, in whole or in part, whether voluntary or by operation of law, except with Author's prior written consent.

This constitutes the entire Agreement between Editor and Author and supersedes any other understandings or terms, including those expressed in any invoice of Editor. This Agreement may not be modified except in writing signed by both parties.

This Agreement will be interpreted and construed in accordance with the law of the State of Connecticut, and shall be governed by and construed in accordance with the law of Connecticut, which shall have exclusive jurisdiction with regard to any claims arising hereunder.

If this Agreement is acceptable, all parties shall sign all copies of the Agreement and return all three (3) copies to Editor at the above address for full execution. A fully executed agreement will be returned to the Author upon execution.

AGREED AND ACCEPTED:
By: _____   By: _____

Departments in Traditional Publishing Companies

The key departments for any traditionally published author are:
Editorial,
Sales,
Subsidiary Rights (Domestic and Foreign Rights Departments),
Special Sales,
Permissions,
Marketing,
Publicity,
Art/Design.

Once a major publisher or even a small press publishes you, you are in competition with all the other authors published by this publishing company. You need to stand out of the crowd and have the back office staff work behind the scene in these Departments for your book.

For example, a Permissions Editor or Permissions Manager will grant excerpts from your book to other Publishers, Authors, in print and online. This is important income for you, which is generally split 50/50 with your publisher (after you earn out your advance).
Subsidiary Rights Departments handle the licensing of audio rights, electronic rights, book club rights, serial rights (magazine excerpts), paperback and reprint rights, large print rights, and foreign rights. Similar to Permissions, this is additional income for you and an additional outlet for publicity exposure in different market areas. Marketing and Publicity departments may offer creative marketing ideas. Publicity will actively mail out your book to obtain reviews and get you noticed in the media. It is vital for your book to get reviews from key sources such as Kirkus Reviews, Publisher's Weekly, New York Times Book Reviews, Library Journal and other major publications or magazines/websites with an significant readership for your particular book. You can never neglect the cover and interior design for your book and the Art Director and Graphic Designers on staff will select the look and typeface for your book, as well as obtain an artist to create artwork for the cover/inside of the book. Of course, it all starts with Editorial and your agent's job is to match your book with the right editor who is enthusiastic and passionate about editing your book before it goes into Copyediting.

BEST ADVICE: Find out all the staff members in these key departments and send thank you notes, holiday cards, chocolate/flowers and demonstrate genuine appreciation for their work. Remember, you are now in competition with all the frontlist and backlist authors in their publishing companies.

A Writer's Checklist
While You're Writing, Consider The Following

☐ The title must entice the reader.

☐ Your voice must shine through your writing.

☐ Consider your tone and writing style.

☐ Themes – consider your themes and moral lessons.

☐ Character Development – consider emotional development & character transformation.

☐ Dialogue – Make sure you follow all rules of correct dialogue creation.

☐ Setting – Place and time require details and imagery.

☐ Include dramatic action.

☐ Create conflicts, tension and suspense.

☐ Create climaxes.

☐ Maintain an appropriate Point of View.

☐ Plots & Subplots – Lead, Objective, Confrontation, and Knockout.

☐ Flashbacks & Foreshadowing.

☐ Track your scenes to insure that you maintain time and place.

☐ Structure of the story – Beginning/Middle/End.

☐ Transitions – Move smoothly from one chapter to the next.

☐ Hook the Reader!

☐ Remember to maintain proper tense throughout (Present or Past).

☐ Outline your novel to help you keep track of your story line & where it's heading.

Self-Publishing Checklist

☐ Research the Competition
☐ Edit and Copyedit Final Version of your Manuscript
☐ Start collecting quotes from published authors
☐ US Copyright Office - copyright the book
☐ ISBN, barcode number (Bowker)
☐ Publishing Company - LLC or publish under your name
☐ Publishing Company - Apply for tax permit#/Federal ID#
☐ Proofread your book one last time for errors and a final read before you print
☐ Find Book Printer via Literary Marketplace Volume Two or online
  ☐ Negotiate an agreement with the printer for costs, due dates, type of paper, binding, send manuscript to them electronically
  ☐ Cover and interior design. You will need a Work-for-Hire Agreement for cover art or interior design
☐ Consider crossmarketing web links on your website or blog
☐ Create email lists of potential book buyers, and send out an email to them
☐ Google Book Search is an excellent tool for promoting your book
☐ Send your book for reviews: Publishers Weekly, Kirkus & Library Journal
☐ Market on the web via: Facebook, LinkedIn, Goodreads, Google+, etc.
☐ Hold special events at libraries, organizations, schools, colleges and bookstores
☐ Consider attending Book Expo America and writers' conferences
☐ Talk to bookstores about arranging for an in-store signing

Marketing Plan / Marketing Platform

The purpose of a marketing plan is to promote and sell books. If it is an organized strategy, it will bring attention to your book by using many different approaches and tactics.

An important first step in a successful marketing plan is obtaining great reviews from Amazon and Barnes & Noble, as well as quotes from published authors in your genre. Quotes will go on the inside of your book, or on the back cover.

Reviews by Publisher's Weekly, Library Journal and Kirkus Review are essential as they are key magazines in the publishing industry. If your book is being traditionally published, your Book Publisher will cover the cost of these reviews. If you are self-published, you will be paying for reviews by Publisher's Weekly, Library Journal and Kirkus Review.

Below is the customized marketing plan created by Jan L. Kardys and Jeanne E. Rogers, Authors of *You Wrote A Book, Now What?* It was created to attract this book's target audience, specifically authors and writers, who are interested in learning more about the publishing business.

How you create your marketing plan depends on many factors including the genre of your book and your targeted audience.

1. Write ads on book to place in Writer's Digest, Poets & Writers and other print/online magazines
2. Brochure with excerpts from book - designed by Annie Sadlon of Sandy Hook, CT and brochure printed in China
3. Mail brochure and reviews to bookstores and libraries in 10 states
4. Mail brochure and reviews to CAPA members, and past attendees of *UNICORN WRITERS' CONFERENCE*
5. Burn DVD with one of our library events or MEETUP group
6. Write articles about publishing journey for various magazines and newspapers
7. Network at various writers' conferences
8. Film book excerpts - put on our website and YouTube
9. Create a PowerPoint about book publishing

The following checklist applies to both traditionally and self-published authors. Use the checklist to help you organize a successful marketing plan:

☐   1. Website

Design your site on paper, then find a web programmer and publish your site. Tabs must include: About, The Book, Events, and Contact. Social media share buttons should appear on every page. You can have Podcasts, YouTube, Audio, and/or Video links embedded on your web pages.

☐   2. Blog

A blog is an interactive website. It is important to share news, events, interesting information your book. To get maximum exposure and build a following from the public, you must consistently publish weekly or monthly. You can market your book by embedding Podcasts, YouTube, Audio, and/or Video links on your web pages.

☐   3. Internet

Write articles for Author's groups and writer's help sites.

☐   4. Emails

Send out an email blast via iContact, Mailchimp, Constant Contact or other bulk email providers.

☐   5. Print

Create a press release, write articles relative to writing and tie in the book – target local papers & online sites.
Do postcards, bookmarks, and brochure on book.
Create flyers, with printed excerpts.

☐   6. Social Media

Google+
Facebook
Twitter
Goodreads
LinkedIn -and many more.

☐   7. TV

Contact Local TV stations, Better CT station.

☐   8. Radio

Obtain a list of local radio stations and call.
Send recorded radio interview to various radio stations.

☐ 9. Special Events

Library Presentation on *You Wrote a Book, Now What?*
Create a presentation on SELF-PUBLISHING VS. TRADITIONAL PUBLISHING
Line up bookstore events on SELF-PUBLISHING VS. TRADITIONAL PUBLISHING
Attend Writer's Conferences
Contact Colleges
Contact MEETUP GROUPS in New England and other states
Contact various writers groups with an announcement about our new book and offer comments in the chat rooms

☐ 10. Launch Party

Book signing launch party at a local restaurant
Contact writers group - Danbury, Redding, Bethel, Wilton, Newtown

☐ 11. Promotion

Purchase car magnet, calendar magnet, unicorn chocolates, print and online ads, etc.

Form TX
For a Nondramatic Literary Work
UNITED STATES COPYRIGHT OFFICE

REGISTRATION NUMBER

Copyright Office fees are subject to change.
For current fees, check the Copyright Office
website at www.copyright.gov, write the Copyright Office, or call (202) 707-3000.

TX _____ TXU _____

EFFECTIVE DATE OF REGISTRATION

Month _____ Day _____ Year _____

DO NOT WRITE ABOVE THIS LINE. IF YOU NEED MORE SPACE, USE A SEPARATE CONTINUATION SHEET.

1 TITLE OF THIS WORK ▼

You Wrote A Book, Now What? Insiders Info on Book Publishing

PREVIOUS OR ALTERNATIVE TITLES ▼

PUBLICATION AS A CONTRIBUTION If this work was published as a contribution to a periodical, serial, or collection, give information about the collective work in which the contribution appeared. **Title of Collective Work ▼**

If published in a periodical or serial give: Volume ▼ _____ Number ▼ _____ Issue Date ▼ _____ On Pages ▼ _____

2

a NAME OF AUTHOR ▼
Jan L. Kardys

DATES OF BIRTH AND DEATH
Year Born ▼ *6/12/1954* Year Died ▼ *-*

Was this contribution to the work a "work made for hire"?
☐ Yes
☑ No

AUTHOR'S NATIONALITY OR DOMICILE
Name of Country
OR { Citizen of *USA*
{ Domiciled in _____

WAS THIS AUTHOR'S CONTRIBUTION TO THE WORK
Anonymous? ☐ Yes ☑ No
Pseudonymous? ☐ Yes ☑ No

If the answer to either of these questions is "Yes," see detailed instructions.

NOTE
Under the law, the "author" of a "work made for hire" is generally the employer, not the employee (see instructions). For any part of this work that was "made for hire" check "Yes" in the space provided, give the employer (or other person for whom the work was prepared) as "Author" of that part, and leave the space for dates of birth and death blank.

NATURE OF AUTHORSHIP Briefly describe nature of material created by this author in which copyright is claimed. ▼
book on book publishing, traditional and self publishing

b NAME OF AUTHOR ▼
Jeanne E. Rogers

DATES OF BIRTH AND DEATH
Year Born ▼ *1/21/1951* Year Died ▼ *-*

Was this contribution to the work a "work made for hire"?
☐ Yes
☑ No

AUTHOR'S NATIONALITY OR DOMICILE
Name of Country
OR { Citizen of *USA*
{ Domiciled in _____

WAS THIS AUTHOR'S CONTRIBUTION TO THE WORK
Anonymous? ☐ Yes ☑ No
Pseudonymous? ☐ Yes ☑ No

If the answer to either of these questions is "Yes," see detailed instructions.

NATURE OF AUTHORSHIP Briefly describe nature of material created by this author in which copyright is claimed. ▼
book on book publishing, traditional and self publishing

c NAME OF AUTHOR ▼

DATES OF BIRTH AND DEATH
Year Born ▼ Year Died ▼

Was this contribution to the work a "work made for hire"?
☐ Yes
☐ No

AUTHOR'S NATIONALITY OR DOMICILE
Name of Country
OR { Citizen of _____
{ Domiciled in _____

WAS THIS AUTHOR'S CONTRIBUTION TO THE WORK
Anonymous? ☐ Yes ☐ No
Pseudonymous? ☐ Yes ☐ No

If the answer to either of these questions is "Yes," see detailed instructions.

NATURE OF AUTHORSHIP Briefly describe nature of material created by this author in which copyright is claimed. ▼

3

a YEAR IN WHICH CREATION OF THIS WORK WAS COMPLETED *2014* Year
This information must be given in all cases.

b DATE AND NATION OF FIRST PUBLICATION OF THIS PARTICULAR WORK
Complete this information ONLY if this work has been published.
Month _____ Day _____ Year _____ Nation _____

4 COPYRIGHT CLAIMANT(S) Name and address must be given even if the claimant is the same as the author given in space 2. ▼
Jan L. Kardys + Jeanne E. Rogers
P.O. Box 176
Redding, CT 06876

See instructions before completing this space.

TRANSFER If the claimant(s) named here in space 4 is (are) different from the author(s) named in space 2, give a brief statement of how the claimant(s) obtained ownership of the copyright. ▼

APPLICATION RECEIVED

ONE DEPOSIT RECEIVED

TWO DEPOSITS RECEIVED

FUNDS RECEIVED

DO NOT WRITE HERE OFFICE USE ONLY

MORE ON BACK ▶ · Complete all applicable spaces (numbers 5-9) on the reverse side of this page.
· See detailed instructions. · Sign the form at line 8.

DO NOT WRITE HERE

Page 1 of _____ pages

Copyright Form

DO NOT WRITE ABOVE THIS LINE. IF YOU NEED MORE SPACE, USE A SEPARATE CONTINUATION SHEET.

PREVIOUS REGISTRATION Has registration for this work, or for an earlier version of this work, already been made in the Copyright Office?

□ Yes ☑ No If your answer is "Yes," why is another registration being sought? (Check appropriate box.) ▼

a. □ This is the first published edition of a work previously registered in unpublished form.

b. ☑ This is the first application submitted by this author as copyright claimant.

c. □ This is a changed version of the work, as shown by space 6 on this application.

If your answer is "Yes," give: **Previous Registration Number** ▶   **Year of Registration** ▶

5

DERIVATIVE WORK OR COMPILATION

Preexisting Material Identify any preexisting work or works that this work is based on or incorporates. ▼

Material Added to This Work Give a brief, general statement of the material that has been added to this work and in which copyright is claimed. ▼

a **6** b

See instructions before completing this space.

DEPOSIT ACCOUNT If the registration fee is to be charged to a Deposit Account established in the Copyright Office, give name and number of Account.

Name ▼   **Account Number** ▼

a **7** b

CORRESPONDENCE Give name and address to which correspondence about this application should be sent. Name / Address / Apt / City / State / Zip ▼

Jan L. Kardys, P.O. Box 176, Redding, CT 06876

203-938-7405

Area code and daytime telephone number ▶   Fax number ▶

Email ▶ unicorn4writers@gmail.com

CERTIFICATION* I, the undersigned, hereby certify that I am the

Check only one ▶

□ author
□ other copyright claimant
□ owner of exclusive right(s)
☑ authorized agent of Jan L. Kardys + Jeanne E. Rogers

of the work identified in this application and that the statements made by me in this application are correct to the best of my knowledge.

Name of author or other copyright claimant, or owner of exclusive right(s) ▲

8

Typed or printed name and date ▼ If this application gives a date of publication in space 3, do not sign and submit it before that date.

Jan L. Kardys   Date ▶ Sept 8, 2014

Handwritten signature ▼

Jan L. Kardys

Certificate will be mailed in window envelope to this address:

Name ▼ Jan L. Kardys

Number/Street/Apt ▼ P.O. Box 176

City/State/Zip ▼ Redding, CT 06876

YOU MUST:
· Complete all necessary spaces
· Sign your application in space 8

SEND ALL 3 ELEMENTS IN THE SAME PACKAGE:
1. Application form
2. Nonrefundable filing fee in check or money order payable to *Register of Copyrights*
3. Deposit material

MAIL TO:
Library of Congress
Copyright Office
101 Independence Avenue SE
Washington, DC 20559-6222

9

Certificate of Registration

Certificate of Registration

This Certificate issued under the seal of the Copyright Office in accordance with title 17, *United States Code*, attests that registration has been made for the work identified below. The information on this certificate has been made a part of the Copyright Office records.

Maria A. Pallante

Register of Copyrights, United States of America

Registration Number

TX 7-802-365

Effective date of registration:

November 5, 2013

Title

Title of Work: The Sword Of Demelza

Completion/Publication

Year of Completion: 2013

Date of 1st Publication: April 5, 2013   **Nation of 1st Publication:** United States

International Standard Number: ISBN   9780615709949

Author

Author: Jeanne Elizabeth Rogers

Pseudonym: J. E. Rogers

Author Created: text

Citizen of: United States

Year Born: 1951

Copyright claimant

Copyright Claimant: Jeanne Elizabeth Rogers

2701 Eaton Court, Danbury, CT, 06811, United States

Certification

Name: Jeanne E. Rogers

Date: September 28, 2013

Applicant's Tracking Number: TSoD

Meet the Authors

Jan L. Kardys has a diverse book publishing career with executive positions at ten of the major book publishers - Doubleday, St. Martin's Press, Scholastic, Macmillan, Charles Scribner's Sons, Little, Brown & Company, Warner Books, Harcourt Brace Jovanovich, Lippincott & Crowell, Publishers, Simon & Schuster/ Prentice Hall, and Condé Nast Publications. Jan also worked for Google for three years and has Internet sales and marketing experience. Her publishing experiences are in editorial, art/production, subsidiary rights, contracts, copyrights, permissions, book agenting, editing, and marketing. Currently, Jan is a literary agent at her Black Hawk Literary Agency (www.JanKardys.com), and creator/Chairman of Unicorn Writers' Conference (www.unicornwritersconference.com). Unicorn Writers' Conference is attended by writers from all over the US and Canada. It is held at Reid Castle, Manhattanville College, in Purchase, NY.

Jan also teaches a class entitled, "Getting Published Today" at continuing education programs, writers' conferences, colleges, and library events.

Jeanne E. Rogers is the self-published author of a Writer's Digest award winning middle grade fantasy, *The Sword of Demelza.* She has successfully plotted a course through the difficult and sometimes frustrating world of writing and publishing. This course includes familiarity with all aspects of social media necessary to create an author platform, successfully self-publish and then market a book. She is active on *Facebook, Linked In, Twitter, Pinterest, Goodreads* and others. Her experience with self-publishing via *CreateSpace*, both in book and eBook format, has provided her with invaluable experience that she is happy to share with her fellow writers. A prolific reader, Jeanne takes great pleasure in writing reviews both publically and privately. She takes the time to read books that are independently or traditionally published, and prepares in-depth reviews, which she then posts to *Amazon*, and *Goodreads*, as well as her own blog – *Australian Fantasy Adventures*, http://warriorechidna.blogspot.com. She can also be found at https://facebook.com/australian-fantasyadventures, *Twitter*, http://twitter.com/warriorechidna, *Pinterest*, http://pinterest.com/warrior echidna, and *LinkedIn*, http://www.linkedin.com/pub/jeanne-e-rogers-author/30/989/2a5/ . She also enjoys privately critiquing pages and first drafts whenever requested from her fellow independent writers. As a result of her experience in self-publishing, and the copyright/trademark world, Jeanne has a working knowledge of the many choices and difficulties new writers face while attempting to focus a spotlight on their work. She is always delighted to work with and help aspiring writers reach their goals by passing on her knowledge and information.

Jan and Jeanne have now combined their talent and experience by establishing *Unicorn for Writers*, (http://unicornforwriters.com), a company devoted to helping writers with all aspects of the writing and publishing process from researching their competition to seeing their manuscript in print. They can be contacted at: **unicorn4writers@gmail.com**.

Jan L. Kardys, left
Jeanne E. Rogers, right

Image Credits

Recommended Books To Read:

- On Writing, by Stephen King

- Bryson's Dictionary for Writers, by Bill Bryson

- Writing Science Fiction and Fantasy, by Crawford Kilian

- The Little Red Writing Book, by Brandon Royal

- Words Fail Me, by Patricia T. O'Connor

- The Elements of Style, by Strunk and White

- Eats, Shoots & Leaves, by Lynne Truss

- The Everyday Writer, by Andrea Lunsford and Robert Connors

- A Writer's Guide To Book Publishing, by Richard Balkin

- Novel Voices
- Edited by Jennifer Levasseur and Kevin Rabalais

- 100 Words Every Word Lover Should Know
- Editors of the American Heritage Dictionaries

- Thinking Like Your Editor, by Suan Rabiner and Alfred Fortunato

- Writing Tools, by Roy Peter Clark

- Bird By Bird, by Anne Lamott

- Rules For Writers, by Diana Hacker

- On Writing Well, by William Zinsser

- The Fire In Fiction, by Donald Maass

- Beginnings, Middles & Ends, by Nancy Kress

- The Art Of War For Writers, by James Scott Bell

- The Plot Whisperer, by Alderson

Recommended Reading, Continued:

THE FOLLOWING ARE QUITE GOOD AND AVAILABLE THROUGH WRITERS DIGEST'S WEBSITE:

(http://www.writersdigestshop.com/?cid=3&gclid=
CN7tma2Ijb0CFSwdOgodszQAHA)

- What Would Your Character Do? by Eric Maisel, Ph.D. and Ann Maisel

- Showing and Telling, by Laurie Alberts

- Characters, Emotion & Viewpoint, by Nancy Kress

FINIS.